A GUIDE TO TREASURE IN

NEVADA

By Thomas Penfield

Cover Illustration by Eugene Shortridge

TRUE TREASURE LIBRARY

Printed by
CARSON ENTERPRISES, INC
P.O. Drawer 71
Deming, N.M. 88031

ISBN 0-941620-15-8

TREASURE GUIDE SERIES

Other books available from True Treasure Library --

* DIRECTORY OF BURIED OR SUNKEN TREASURES
  AND LOST MINES OF THE UNITED STATES

* A GUIDE TO TREASURE IN NEBR - KANS - NO &
  SO DAKOTA

* A GUIDE TO TREASURE IN CALIFORNIA

* A GUIDE TO TREASURE IN TEXAS

* A GUIDE TO TREASURE IN ARK - LA - MISS

* A GUIDE TO TREASURE IN ARIZONA

* A GUIDE TO TREASURE IN NEVADA

* A GUIDE TO TREASURE IN NEW MEXICO

* A GUIDE TO TREASURE IN MISSOURI

* A GUIDE TO TREASURE IN UTAH

* A GUIDE TO TREASURE IN ILLINOIS AND INDIANA

* A GUIDE TO TREASURE IN MICHIGAN AND OHIO

* A GUIDE TO TREASURE IN PENNSYLVANIA

* A GUIDE TO TREASURE IN VIRGINIA AND WEST
  VIRGINIA

* A GUIDE TO TREASURE IN KENTUCKY

* A GUIDE TO TREASURE IN TENNESSEE

* A GUIDE TO TREASURE IN OKLAHOMA, VOL 1,2,3

FREE! Treasure Reference Catalog.
              Dealer Discounts available.

CARSON ENTERPRISES
Drawer 71, Deming, NM 88031-0071

INTRODUCTION

To many Americans Nevada is a wasteland—a land of burning sand, scrag-gly sagebrush and alkaline sinks, a lonely, desolate land. But surrounding that desert in chain after chain of serrated grandeur, multi-colored mountains rise over priceless deposits of metals and minerals. Pausing only at Reno or Las Vegas, most travelers miss the Nevada of lost mines and hidden treasure.

Nevada was born of mineral discovery. The thin detritus blanket over its mountain slopes aided prospectors in detecting the outcroppings of its ores. The first settlers in the state were the Mormons who came in 1849. In the same year, gold was discovered near Virginia City. In 1859, placer mining on that gulch uncovered the famous Comstock Lode, the richest deposit of precious metals ever found on earth. Overnight Virginia City became the new Eldorado that lured fortune hunters from all over the world.

Prospecting is an insatiable passion in Nevada, and most Nevadans are enchained by it. In a land as highly mineralized as their state there are, of course, tales of fabulous ledges of untold wealth found and lost. These mines have been sought through the years by prospectors following the beckoning finger of hope.

Although few mines, once lost, are ever recovered, the search for rumored gold is often productive. Several mining towns in Nevada have been founded on the site of a discovery made while the prospector was looking for a fabled lost mine. The ghost town of Belmont is of this type, and Tonopah, the greatest boom camp of the 1900's, could almost be called a recovered mine.

A Guide to Treasure in Nevada is another volume in the series which will eventually cover the treasure sites in all fifty states of the Union. The volume is divided into two sections—Treasure Sites and Metal Detector Sites. In both sections, treasure locations are described and listed alphabetically by counties.

A book of this type cannot claim to encompass all the treasure sites in Nevada. Many Nevadans will doubtless mourn the absence of some of their favorite locations which the author's years of careful study and research have failed to disclose.

Metal detector sites classified as ghost towns are those which appeared in the census and on the maps of 1885 but are not included in the latest publications of maps and the census.

Lost mine stories are susceptible to numerous variations. The versions related here are those that seem most pertinent to man's age-long dream of riches that still materialize in the mines of Nevada.

Thomas Penfield
Los Angeles, California
January, 1974

NEVADA

TREASURE SITES

Seekers of lost mines, treasures and relics in Nevada should remember that large sections of the state are reserved for United States bombing, gunnery and nuclear testing. Restricted areas contain some of the lost mine and treasure sites listed here. Though no trespassing is permitted on such government preserves, those sites have been included in order to make this volume as complete as possible.

Clark County—The first Spanish mining in Nevada was probably south of Las Vegas, particularly in Eldorado Canyon. This operation doubtless predated Escalante's expedition of 1776.

The first mining by Americans is believed to have been at Potosi Mountain in the Spring Mountains southwest of Las Vegas. Mormons founded the mining camp of Mountain Springs. By 1855, they were taking out ore which they assumed to be pure lead. They sold it for making bullets in the settlements as far north as Utah. Indian troubles ended their mining activities. Their holdings were eventually acquired and operated by the Colorado Mining Company.

In 1897, two unnamed brothers accompanied by a mule skinner drove a wagon from Utah with supplies for the Mormons remaining in the area. They also brought two chests containing $20,000 in minted silver to invest in the Colorado Mining Company. At Mountain Springs, the three men were attacked by Indians. One brother was killed, and the other two men, both wounded, were left for dead. Some days later, the two survivors were found near death from loss of blood and exposure. Taken to the Colorado Mining Company camp, they were placed in the care of the cook, a Paiute Indian woman. The brother told the woman that just before the attack, he and the mule skinner had taken the two chests of silver coins from the wagon and hidden them behind a large rock. After the attack, when they had regained sufficient strength, they had dug a shallow hole and buried the chests.

The two men died a few days after confiding their secret to the Indian woman. She immediately made a search of the battle site and found the charred remains of the brothers' wagon. Alone and concealing her movements, she dug around the largest rocks in the vicinity but failed to locate the two chests of coins. After revealing the information to others, she was aided in her search, but no treasure is known to have been found.

TREASURE GUIDE

Clark County—About the turn of the century an old Mormon appeared at a mill near the California-Nevada line and sold several burro loads of rich gold-bearing ore. He, of course, did not offer any information about the source of his gold, but it was assumed by prospectors who knew the area that it had come from the foothills of the McCullough Mountains.

Time passed, and eventually the old prospector was back with another load of the same kind of ore. For several months he returned periodically to the mill, made his transaction, and left. Then his visits ceased.

Sometime afterward, a party of cowboys found the Mormon's body on the desert floor. Scattered nearby were remains of his pack animals. It was assumed that he had been murdered for his wealth and the secret to the location of his mine.

Later, the remnants of an old camp were discovered on the west side of the McCullough Range. This could have been the Mormon's camp, but no gold ore was found in the vicinity. The old prospector was doubtless too wily to establish his camp close to his mine, and he would have been careful to conceal the entrance to it. Prospectors still search the McCullough Mountains for the Lost Mormon Mine.

Clark County—One day in 1872, a gold prospector known only as Lawrence arrived at the old O. D. Gass Ranch, now the site of Las Vegas. He left the following morning and traveled in a southeasterly direction toward the Colorado River.

In the volcanic formations characteristic of this country, Lawrence's attention was drawn to a seam of blue "mud" which ran at right angles to the surrounding formation. He carried away a few samples of the substance which he later panned out and recovered a handful of "rocks," or "crystals." He placed these specimens in his knapsack and continued his search for gold.

After carrying the rocks with him for some time, Lawrence asked a jeweler in Los Angeles if they were worth anything. Indeed they were, the jeweler informed him. They were diamonds from one to 3½ carats in weight!

Under the impression that he could return to the seam of blue mud at any time, Lawrence is said to have given the diamonds to friends. But when he went back to wash out more diamonds, the blue seam had vanished. He was never able to locate it again.

Clark County—Goodsprings is an old mining camp at the eastern base of the Spring Mountain Range. Gold, silver, platinum, vanadium and copper were all present here, but of these copper was the most plentiful. One day in the early 1900's, a chemist assaying a shipment of copper ore from the Boss Mine near Goodsprings noted a peculiar reaction to the tests. Further investigation revealed that the ore was rich in platinum. This was not unusual since the district had produced small quantities of platinum. But the value of this ore was far beyond anything previously discovered.

When the owners of the Boss Mine were notified that a yellow-gray substance in their copper was platinum worth $70 to $90 per refined ounce, it raised an important question. Was there also platinum in the mine dump? A test was made which showed the same values as the sample. Immediate steps were taken to recover the fortune that had been cast aside. It is said that a single carload of this dump material yielded $135,000.

Such startling news, of course, precipitated a platinum stampede, and the vicinity around Goodsprings was thoroughly explored. No other platinum, however, was found. The Boss Mine was methodically investigated and worked, but it showed no further trace of platinum. Mining experts decided that one huge pocket had been struck and its supply exhausted.

Some geologists suggest that the platinum in the Boss Mine was only a part of a huge deposit formed centuries ago and that the mother lode is still concealed somewhere in the area.

Clark County—The small town of Searchlight is named for the famous brand of Searchlight matches. According to local legend, two brothers camped here in 1898. One of them looked at the brand on his box of matches, lighted the campfire and called the place Searchlight. The region is highly mineralized and the scene of many mining stories. One of these concerns the sale of a mine for a team of mules, a buckboard and a shotgun. The mine later produced more than $1,000,000. Another that brought its owner $150,000 had changed hands for a pint of whiskey!

The Lost Skillet Mine near Searchlight was discovered by a mining engineer looking for a suitable campsite. He came upon shallow diggings, investigated and found nothing. But near the excavation he dug out a half-buried skillet filled with fabulously rich gold ore. Examining a nearby ledge, he saw the same type of ore as that in the skillet. After thoroughly exploring the neighborhood, he concluded that he had stumbled upon a valuable find which had been previously worked. He gathered a generous supply of samples, covered the exposed ore, carefully marked the spot, and left. Sometime later, he outfitted himself and started out to work his new find. But when he returned to the place he thought was the ledge of gold, he was unable to locate a single marker. He spent years searching in the region then gave up. The Lost Skillet Mine is still lost.

Clark County—A German Mormon named Mashbird once stopped at the Gass Ranch, which is now Las Vegas. Shortly thereafter, he and a companion left on a prospecting trip in the mountains to the southwest. About a month later, Mashbird stumbled back to the ranch, suffering from a head wound and muttering incoherently that he had been attacked by an Indian and his companion killed.

After being nursed back to health, Mashbird was able to fill in the details of his story. He said that he and his partner had gone into the McCullough Mountains where they had camped near a spring. From here they made leisurely prospecting trips into the surrounding country. One day, an Indian came to their camp and accepted the prospectors' invitation to have a meal with them. The Indian assured them that he knew where there was much gold a short distance away and offered to take them there.

Mashbird went with him while the companion remained at the camp. On the trail, the Indian fell behind the German, suddenly attacked him with a stone, and left him for dead. Mashbird, however, returned to consciousness, and despite his injury decided to see if the Indian had been lying to him about the gold. A short distance farther down the faint trail, he found a rich deposit of horn silver with free gold.

His pockets filled with specimens, Mashbird staggered back to the camp where he saw his companion lying dead and the place stripped of their provisions. Somehow, he managed to make his way back to the Gass Ranch. He searched many months for the dim path and the gold, but never found it.

Clark County—A prospector from North Carolina had come to Nevada on his doctor's advice. While traveling one day from Crescent to Searchlight in the extreme southern corner of the state, he thought he saw from the slopes of Clark Mountain a large body of water. His canteens needed refilling, but he turned in that direction only to find a mirage.

Climbing a hill that rose out of the ancient lake bed, he saw the entrance to a cave. He entered it cautiously. After following a tunnel-like passage for some distance, he heard the sound of running water. Proceeding farther, he came to a vast room from the edge of which he looked down upon a boiling mass of water. As he stood enthralled at the sight, the water slowly receded revealing terraced walls leading down to a basin-like bottom which was covered with black sand. Carefully working his way down to the bottom, the prospector examined the sand and found that it was filled with gold nuggets. He picked up all he could carry and climbed the terraced wall. When he reached the large room, he turned and looked down again at the black sand. Pondering the strange disappearance of the water, he concluded that its rise and fall was actually the Pacific tide reaching the cavern through some great subterranean system and bringing with it great fresh quantities of gold every 24 hours. The abundance of gold that could be obtained here staggered his imagination.

But he was on his way to see a doctor in Searchlight. He left the cave and continued across the desert wastes. In Searchlight, he told the story of the cave of gold to other prospectors. Not long after this, the North Carolinian disappeared and was never seen again. Nor has anyone ever found the cave he described.

Not more than 30 or 40 airline miles northwest of this supposed cave of gold, another immense cavern is reported to be filled with black sand and studded with gold nuggets. In this place too, the ocean tides sweep in and out with lunar regularity. It has been suggested that these two caverns may be connected and that the golden sands stretch from one to the other. It has also been suggested that both stories are the result of overworked imaginations.

Clark County—Devil's Peak rises abruptly from the flat desert floor southeast of the old mining camp of Goodsprings near the California line. It was a noted landmark to earlyday travelers.

Although no reference to the incident can be documented, tradition says that the bodies of five men were once found at the base of Devil's Peak. At the time, the report was that they were on their way from San Bernadino to Las Vegas, prospecting the country as they traveled.

In the vicinity of Devil's Peak, the five men are said to have discovered gold-bearing ore. Presumably, they quarreled over the division of this ore, and a gunfight ensued in which all were either killed or died soon afterwards of wounds. Several days later, their bodies were found, and scattered about them was the large quantity of gold and silver ore they had gathered. This ore was later assayed and ran $1,000 to the ton.

Nevadans say that prospectors are still searching for the source of this ore.

Clark County—Not far distant from Eldorado, also known as Nelson, sometime early in 1940, a prospector stumbled upon a man-made barricade in front of a shallow cave on the face of a high canyon wall. Inside the cave he discovered the skeleton of an Indian, and scattered around him were a loaded shotgun, steel-tipped arrows, a bullet mold and other odds and ends. Authorities called from Las Vegas identified the skeleton as that of an Indian named Quejo who for more than 10 years had terrorized people living in remote sections of Clark County.

There are several contradictory stories of Quejo's origin and early years. One is that he was a Paiute. Another is that he belonged to an Arizona tribe and lived for a time with Paiutes on the Nevada side of the Colorado. One story has it that he started his career of crime by murdering a tribal member over a dispute about a medicine man's techniques. Shortly afterward, he attacked Hi Bohn of Las Vegas and broke both his arms. Another story says that he was ordered by authorities to track down one of his brothers who was a killer and bring back his head as proof of the deed.

But Quejo's known history starts in 1910 when he killed a guard at the Gold Bug Mine near Eldorado. He was linked to other crimes by his footprints which had certain striking irregularities. For several years his trail was obscured, but he was blamed for the disappearance of several lone prospectors. Near Eldorado in 1919, he was stealing food from the home of Ned Douglas when Ned's wife walked into the kitchen. Quejo shot and killed the woman. This aroused high feeling in the community, and the same men who had trailed the Indian in 1910 were commissioned to capture him. They tracked him up the Colorado River to St. Thomas, now buried by an arm of Lake Mead, across the Colorado to the Arizona side, and back down the river where he again crossed to the Nevada side.

Near St. Thomas, two prospectors had been killed in savage style, and two days later two men and two boys were found murdered on the opposite side of the river near Black Canyon. Seven killings in all took place at that time, and Quejo's peculiar footprints showed clearly on the ground near all the bodies.

Numbers of men from Arizona and Nevada spent months following Quejo's tracks. The sheriff of Clark County, finding campfires not yet cold, knew that he was close to him on several occasions. One night, the sheriff found hismelf trapped in a box canyon and was so certain that the Indian would kill him that he wrote his name on a cliff above the spot where he lay down to sleep so that his body could be identified. But Quejo disappeared and there was no clue to his fate until his bones were found in the shallow cave.

All that was lacking here for an exciting treasure story was the treasure, but this did not deter a Hollywood television producer then making a series on lost mines and buried treasure. A member of the camera crew learned the Quejo story and proposed to make a "treasure" film of it. He was given permission and took some scenes of the cave with its identifying articles which he found still preserved in Las Vegas. He put everything together with superficial narration and passed it off on television viewers as the "**Treasure of Quejo's Cave.**" If there is, or ever was, any treasure in Quejo's Cave, no one has found it.

Churchill County—About 1880, Henry Knight prospected the Painted Hills, a small range near Sand Springs, and located a minor vein of gold. Tracing this vein, he came to a place that looked promising and sank a shaft. At about 50 feet, he broke into an opening that turned out to be a cave the walls of which were lined with free gold. As he dug in the walls, more gold appeared. He did not take time to investigate the full extent of his find.

Working hard to prepare some of the ore to be taken out, he suddenly begin to feel ill and emerged from the cave for a breath of fresh air. When the illness persisted, he left the gold and went to Sand Springs to see a doctor.

Knight never recovered. Although he told the doctor about his cave, he gave only vague directions as to its location, and the gold was lost.

Churchill County—Sand Springs is now no more than a site on US Highway 50 about 23 miles east of Fallon. When it was an important station on a stage line, a Shoshone Indian staggered into the settlement one day carrying an extremely rich piece of quartz. He was very ill, but before he died he tried to tell where he had found the quartz. His description led to the belief that the location was in the lower reaches of the Stillwater Range. For many years, prospectors searched for the Shoshone Lost Ledge, but today it is practically forgotten.

Douglas County—In 1861, a sawmill was built in Glenbrook on Lake

Tahoe, and the town became an important lumber shipping point to supply the Comstock mines. In March of 1891, Zeb Walters, a Wells Fargo messenger, picked up the payroll for the Tahoe-Glenbrook Lumber Company in Carson City and prepared to deliver it to Glenbrook. A fierce snowstorm was raging, but Walters was a dedicated man and he knew how much those men at Glenbrook wanted their pay. The money amounted to $12,000 in freshly-minted, uncirculated coins from the Carson City Mint—500 double Eagles and 200 Eagles.

At Flume House, Walters left the stage and transferred his box of gold coins to the caboose of the narrow-gauge railroad for the remainder of the trip into Glenbrook. He placed the chest at his feet and settled down for a comfortable trip. There was little reason to worry about a robbery in this kind of weather. Before reaching Glenbrook, Walters transferred the chest to the tender to be a bit closer to his destination at the end of the run.

On the small dock in Glenbrook, the locomotive's brakes failed. Train, tender, Zeb Walters and his chest of gold all tumbled into the icy waters of Lake Tahoe. Zeb managed to throw himself clear of the tender and was pulled out of the water, but his chest of gold was gone. When warm weather came, two expert divers searched for the treasure. But the chest had slipped off a steep ledge and was beyond their reach in 90 feet of water. Repeated attempts to salvage the chest of gold have failed, but it is there—in some of the coldest water in the United States.

Douglas County—The largest casino robbery in Nevada gambling history occurred when Harrah's Lake Tahoe Resort in Stateline was robbed of $178,500 in 1972. The FBI recovered $126,280 in the Lake Tahoe area in September of that year, but the remaining $52,220 has not been found. The four men arrested and convicted of the crime have consistently refused to reveal where the money was hidden. It is believed to be in the vicinity of Lake Tahoe, probably near Stateline.

Douglas County—The town of Genoa was known as Mormon Station until 1855. Established when this region was in western Utah, it is the oldest permanent settlement in Nevada. In 1855, it was the seat of Carson County, Utah Territory. In 1861, it became the seat of Douglas County, Nevada, and retained that position until 1916. Genoa's early prosperity and growth came from the rush of miners from California to Virginia City, and the mining at Virginia City created an immense amount of freight and stagecoach travel through the town.

The vast amount of bullion shipped out of the Comstock Mines to Carson City and San Francisco made the road from Genoa to Virginia City the scene of innumerable stagecoach robberies.

Just outside Genoa at the height of the gold-mining period, two highwaymen stopped a stagecoach and seized a whiskey keg packed with $20,000 in gold coins destined for Virginia City to meet mining payrolls.

TREASURE GUIDE

Knowing that a posse would soon be on their trail, and finding the keg of coins too heavy to transport on horseback, the robbers buried the treasure at the base of a pine tree. They then made a pact declaring that the treasure would not be touched for six months, after which it could be recovered and spent at leisure without attracting attention. But one of the outlaws returned to the site, dug up the treasure, rolled it to another tree, and reburied it. Meantime, his accomplice, identified by the stagecoach passengers, was taken by a posse and promptly hanged.

The surviving bandit fled to Colorado where he prospered in mining ventures. Years later, when he was bankrupt, he returned to Genoa and made a search for the keg of coins but was unable to locate it. During this time he became ill. Before his death he told of the buried gold and gave its location as nearly as he could recall. Soon afterward, a land slide swept down the mountain into Genoa, killing a number of people and causing great damage. The spot the bandit had named as the repository of his treasure must have been covered by the landslide, for the keg of gold has never been found.

Elko County—The last stagecoach robbery in the west is believed to have been at Jarbidge, Nevada, December 5, 1916. It is an intriguing tale of treasure, a small one but one that is perfectly documented.

Snow was falling that December evening, and already three to four feet had accumulated on Crippen Grade which led down a precipitous wall into Jarbidge Canyon where a booming camp was snuggled along the bank of Jarbidge River. Heavy snows in this most isolated of all Nevada mining camps was nothing unusual. Sometimes the town was cut off from the outside world for weeks by 30-foot drifts.

Despite the storm, a small group of men gathered at the post office to await the arrival of the stagecoach from Rogerson, Idaho, some 60 miles to the north. Everyone assumed that Fred Searcy, the driver, would be late, and nobody envied him his job that night. The road he had to travel dropped 2,000 feet in the five and one-half miles from Jarbidge Summit to the bottom of the canyon, and it frequently gave the impression of terminating in space.

Hours passed, and Searcy had had time to arrive even in the snowstorm. Postmaster Scott Fleming, who was expecting a registered mail pouch, became alarmed and asked Frank Leonard to ride to the top of the grade to look for the stagecoach. When Leonard returned several hours later and reported that he had seen nothing of Searcy, there was deep concern for his safety. His vehicle could easily slide off the slippery canyon road and roll into the river.

Fleming telephoned Rose Dexter, who lived close to the road a half mile from the north edge of town. She informed him that she had seen the stagecoach pass her door hours ago. She had, in fact, been in her yard to get some wood and had waved at the driver who sat huddled on his seat with his coat collar pulled over his face as if he were half-frozen.

Fleming and a search party carrying lanterns trudged up the road through the storm. In a short time, they came upon the stagecoach less than a quarter of a mile from the town's main business section. It was pulled off the road and almost concealed in a clump of willows to which the shivering horses were tied. Slumped in his seat and almost covered with snow was the driver, Fred Searcy. When he failed to answer their calls, the searchers assumed that he was frozen. But a closer examination revealed that he had been shot in the head and at such close range that his hair was powder burned. Near the stagecoach, someone kicked something out of the snow that proved to be the first-class mail pouch, unopened. But the registered pouch, containing $4,000 in cash, was nowhere to be seen.

The increasing fury of the storm halted further search that night, but guards were posted at the two canyon outlets to the town and an all-night vigil was organized. On the following morning, the crime was reconstructed from the only evidence available. It was obvious that the robber had swung aboard the slow-moving stage a short distance past Rose Dexter's house and killed Searcy. He then took the reins and continued down the grade. Pulling off the road into the willows, he had rifled the registered mail pouch and propped the dead man up on the driver's seat in a normal position.

Careful investigation revealed a man's dim footprints in the snow. Along with the footprints were the unmistakable paw prints of a large dog. Slowly they were trailed down to the river, where a discarded blood-stained shirt was found. The tracks then crossed the small bridge into the town and disappeared.

Up to this point, nobody had thought anything about the old town dog that had tagged along throughout the investigation. He belonged to nobody in particular but was friendly with everyone. Suddenly, the dog loped off playfully and sniffed at a mound of snow as if he had known all the time that something was there. It was the missing registered mail pouch, slit open and emptied of its $4,000. Was this the dog that had accompanied the murderer during the commission of his crime? His paws were compared to the dim tracks in the night's snow and seemed to fit perfectly. Whom would the dog be likely to follow in a snowstorm?

Everyone knew that the old dog was especially fond of a miner named Ben Kuhl, a man who was unpopular in the camp. He was free on bond at the time, appealing a $400 fine for claim-jumping. This was enough to point the finger of suspicion at Kuhl. He was arrested in his cabin, charged with the murder of Fred Searcy, and accused of robbing the US Mail.

He was brought to trial at Elko, the county seat. Steadfastly professing his innocence, he claimed that he had spent the evening of the murder in a Jarbidge saloon. Several witnesses swore that he had, indeed, been in the saloon. But upon cross-examination, they admitted they could not be sure that it was the evening of the crime or another evening about that date. Kuhl was sentenced to life imprisonment and taken to the Nevada State Prison at Carson City. He was received on October 17, 1917, as Number

2018, almost a year after the commission of the crime.

Throughout his imprisonment he consistently denied his guilt. On May 7, 1945, he was released on parole, and at this writing, according to Nevada State Prison authorities, he is still alive and in good health. He had no previous prison record and has been in no trouble since his release. Considering this, prison authorities will not reveal his whereabouts, saying only that he has never returned to Jarbidge.

And the $4,000? In denying the crime, Kuhl, of course denied any knowledge of the money. So far as anyone knows, it was never recovered. Apparently, it is still cached there in the canyon at the edge of Jarbidge.

Elko County—In the late 1870's, a party of Mormons did some exploring for suitable farmlands in the upper Jarbidge district. In the course of their travels, two members of the party found placer gold in one of the area's small streams. Since mining was not looked upon with favor by the Mormon leaders in Salt Lake City, the two men kept their find a secret. Upon the completion of their assignment, however, they returned to the Jarbidge country, located their placer find, traced it to its source, and built a small arrastre for grinding the ore.

In their secretive manner the two partners mined and milled their ore, occasionally taking gold to be sold or traded in Elko or Tuscarora. Their trips were infrequent and their purchases small enough not to excite special interest in their appearance. There were too many rich deposits at the time for the find of the two Mormons to attract much attention. Even when their trips to Elko and Tuscarora ceased, their absence was hardly noticed. Men came and went in this wild and rugged country, and nobody asked questions. The two Mormons were never seen again.

Many years later, a stage driver passing through the same general region the Mormons had mined picked up some samples of ore which he left with friends to be assayed. The friends took their time in carrying out the request, and when the report came in revealing the ore to be fabulously rich in gold, the stage driver, had disappeared. He was never seen again, and no one had the slightest idea where his find had been made except that it was someplace in the Jarbidge country.

Slowly, the stories of the discoveries made by the two Mormons and the stage driver began to arouse interest, and the conclusion was drawn that there must be at least one rich deposit of gold ore in the Jarbidge Mountains. Some thought that the stage driver had stumbled upon the same body of ore that had been worked by the two Mormons.

A few miners strayed into the region in search of the lost ore. Among these was a prospector named Ross who came upon a piece of rich float. But since winter was approaching, he decided to get out before being trapped in by heavy snow. He thrust his pick and shovel into the earth to mark the point where he had left the trail of the float and started down the mountain. On the following day, he stopped at a summer sheep camp where a herder named Ishman tended a flock for his employer, John Pence. Ishman invited Ross to remain overnight, and the prospector accepted.

According to local accounts, Ross told Ishman of his find. He described the locality, including the pick and shovel he had left to mark the limits of the float he had traced. He suggested that if he did not return in the spring he would be glad to have the sheepherder continue to search. Ross left the next morning and was never seen again.

When winter came, the herder took his flock to the home ranch. With spring, he was back again at his summer camp. He located the canyon in which Ross had found the float and came upon the pick and shovel stuck in the ground. Nearby, there were some scattered bones picked clean by animals. Piecing these together, Ishman reconstructed the skeleton of a man. There was no way to tell whether this was the remains of Ross or of someone who had stumbled upon his trail. The shepherd took the skull to his camp.

All summer, while grazing his sheep along the canyon, he followed the float piece by piece. Before it was time to move his flock down the mountain for the winter, he had located the main body of ore. It was an outcropping thickly impregnated with gold. The herder collected some samples of the ore, covered the outcropping with brush and dirt, hid the pick and shovel, and returned to the ranch.

He took the ore samples and the skull he had found as proof of his statements and told his story to John Pence. Pence had the samples assayed, and they are said to have shown $4,000 worth of gold to the ton. The two men agreed to keep the find a secret and go to the outcropping the following spring.

In the spring as they climbed into the high country, Pence noticed that Ishman was breathing heavily. Suddenly, he reeled and slumped to the ground. Pence managed to get the stricken man out of the mountains and took him almost 100 miles in a wagon to the nearest doctor. The sheepherder died a few days later without regaining consciousness.

Since he was to lead Pence to the gold, he had never told him its exact location on the mountain, and the secret of the ore was lost. Pence had a vague idea where it was and grubstaked several prospectors to search for it, but none of them were ever successful. The Lost Sheepherder Mine seemed to have vanished. The mystery of the skeleton near it was never solved, nor was the strange disappearance of the two Mormons and the stage driver explained.

There seems little doubt as to the authenticity of this story. It has been handed down by one who knew the sheepherder, and John Pence was not a man to go off on tangents. The mine's general location is in rough, primitive country, the ice box of Nevada, where snow lingers late in the mountain passes and the summers are short.

A letter was published in a treasure magazine in 1971 by a person who wished to be anonymous. In it he stated that he and a Reno prospector had found the Lost Sheepherder Mine in 1931. In the summer of 1932, they had taken out $23,840 in gold. They had covered the remaining vein and left it. Neither of the two men had ever returned to the mine. The writer had gone to Australia and made a fortune in the opal mines. His partner had died. Presumably, the letter said, the mine is intact on the east side of the Bruneau River close to the Idaho border. Even so, it appears that the Lost Sheepherder Mine is still lost.

Elko County—Somewhere in the region of Harrison Pass in the Ruby Mountains, there is said to be an Old Spanish gold mine. Shoshone Indians are believed to know where the mine is, but they will not reveal its location to the white man. Some superstition seems to prevent their working it.

Elko County—In 1864, a party of seven prospectors from Silver City, Idaho, entered the then little known section of northeastern Nevada near the present town of Owyhee. Following the Owyhee River, they reached the Bull Run Mountains. Aware that this was dangerous Indian country, they kept sharp watch throughout their travels. Along McCann Creek at the head of Independence Valley, they discovered rich gold placers in an area that had probably never been prospected. In a short time they gathered 200 pounds of dust and nuggets.

One day when the prospectors were scattered, a band of Shoshone Indians who had been secretly observing them suddenly attacked. Although some of the miners were badly wounded, they all managed to get together. Taking about $100,000 worth of raw gold with them, they gained the crest of a ridge where they entrenched themselves for a last-ditch fight against overwhelming odds. They selected two men to go to Silver City for help. The men succeeded in getting through the Indian lines, but when the rescue party reached the scene of the attack, the other five miners were found dead and the gold was missing. It was assumed that the Indians had taken it.

In 1867, a party of prospectors from Austin, Nevada, was led to the site of the massacre by an old Paiute Indian known only as Captain Jim. On the neighboring eastern slope of Mount Blitzen, the Austin men found gold and silver ore which began the development of a mining district near Tuscarora that produced $40,000,000.

Among the thousands of men attracted to the new golconda were two who had been members of the Silver City rescue party. These two men were determined to find out what had happened to the $100,000 in gold that had belonged to the five massacred miners. The men learned from the Shoshones who had taken part in the attack that no gold had been found on the battlefield. Obviously, the five miners had buried it before they made their last stand. But the spot was never located. It is believed that the buried treasure is still in that vicinity.

NEVADA

Elko County—The now-deserted mining camp of Allegheny was named for an old Indian fighter, George Washington Mardis, better know as "Old Allegheny." Old Allegheny prospected in this section of northeastern Nevada, grew rich, bought a ranch, and settled down to raising horses.

One day in the 1880's, he left Charleston for Elko to deposit $40,000 in gold dust and coins. Near the headwaters of the Bruneau River south of Charleston, he was murdered by a lone highwayman.

Some friends came upon his still-warm body and captured the murderer. The highwayman had no gold and denied that the dead man had any. Since no gold was to be found, only two assumptions could account for the absence of the $40,000 known to have been in Allegheny's possession when he left Charleston. Either the murderer had had time to bury the gold before he was caught, or Old Allegheny, suspicious of the approaching rider, had hurriedly buried it before the murderer overtook him. So far as is known the gold has never been found.

Elko County—John Esterly was a Salt Lake City Mormon with a meager knowledge of mining. For some unknown reason he was banished from Utah. Packing his possessions and three wives on mules, he started for Nevada Territory in defiance of his church's orders. One night the small party made camp near the headwaters of the Humboldt River. Here Esterly became ill. After ten days, he was able to travel again. On the morning of his departure, he was rounding up his mules and came upon a vein of gold— a large wide vein that staggered his imagination with its potential wealth. He gathered a few specimens, made mental notes of the surrounding area, gathered up the straying animals, and proceeded westward to the settlements in Carson Valley.

At Carson City, he had the samples assayed, and they showed an amazing $150,000 to the ton. Such fantastic news could not be kept secret, and soon the whole valley was buzzing with excitement. Esterly's every move was watched lest he slip away without revealing the location of his sensational find. At last, the pressure on him became so great that he agreed to lead a party back over his trail to the vein of gold.

After weeks of unsuccessful searching, however, he admitted that he was completely lost. Some members of the party did not believe him and threatened reprisals for leading them on a wild goose chase. Eventually, the search was abandoned. In the end, Esterly's honesty could no longer be questioned. He searched in vain for years for the lost gold but never found it.

Esmeralda County—When Candelaria was a booming silver camp, the ores from its mines had to be freighted to the mills at Columbus about five miles southeast where there was sufficient salt and water for the milling process. There was constant traffic between these two points, including two stages daily. These stagecoaches frequently carried payrolls for the mines

19

and mills and were the constant targets of highwaymen.

On one occasion, an outlaw stopped the Candelaria-bound stage and seized the payroll it was carrying. Pursued toward Columbus, he managed to bury the loot just before being overtaken at the edge of town. No money was found on him, of course, and as soon as the story spread a concentrated search was made for the plunder. Nothing is known to have been found.

Humboldt County—About 1910, an unnamed cowboy is said to have discovered a rich ledge of gold while riding the range. He later returned with pick and shovel, took out small quantity of ore and left his tools to mark the spot. Apparently, the cowboy took others into his confidence and offered to lead them to the ore. On the morning the party was to leave, a horse kicked the cowboy in the head and the injury proved fatal. Before he died, he described the location of his ledge of gold as best he could, indicating that it was in the Kelly Creek district and marked with his pick and shovel. Kelly Creek was a stream in Humboldt County extending into Elko County on the east side of the Osgood Range.

The marking of a ledge of ore with a pick and shovel is a normal thing to do, but it occurs with such frequency in lost mine stories as to arouse suspicion that the gear for one story is appropriated for another. And, of course, if fatal accidents and sudden death did not happen at the last moment before the location of a mine was revealed, there would be fewer lost mines.

Humboldt County—The Black Rock country of northwestern Nevada is a land known to comparatively few people, yet not many places in the west can equal its great variety of breathtaking scenery. Part of the region is a flat desert floor where mirages shimmer fantastically in the summer sun. But within this same region are multi-colored mountains and valleys, great alkali sinks, craggy forests, twisted fields of lava, and grotesque rock formations. This is the locale of the Lost Hardin Mine, probably the most famous mine in Nevada.

Like other hoary lost mine stories, the Hardin tale is embellished with numerous puzzling versions. Asa Merrill Fairfield, California and Nevada historian, has gathered authentic data on the subject and talked to many men who prospected the Black Rock country. The accounts which follow are based on his exhaustive research, contemporary newspaper reports, and information from people who were intimate with James Allen Hardin.

In the summer of 1849, Hardin was a member of a westbound wagon train that had taken the Lassen Cutoff from Winnemucca, Nevada, instead of following the more popular Humboldt River route that turned southwesterly toward Carson Valley. The train consisted of 14 wagons and 200 persons. Swinging northward, the pioneers followed the trail across a wing of the Black Rock Desert, then clung to the eastern side of its northern wing paralleling the Black Rock Range mountains. The mountain range was named for the huge black rock at its southern end. This bold black peak was a landmark known to all travelers of the region.

North of Black Rock, Hardin's train camped at a place still known as Double Hot Springs, a little oasis at the edge of the desert looking eastward to the Black Rock foothills. Before starting out the next morning, the party decided that Hardin, who acted as a combination scout-hunter for the train, should try his luck at bringing in some game. Some accounts maintain that there were three in his party, but Fairfield records that Andrew Hardin, a nephew of James Allen Hardin, many years afterward said that his uncle was accompanied by one man, John Lambert, who later became superintendent of the Sierra Nevada Mine in Virginia City.

Crossing the sandhills edging the desert, Hardin and Lambert followed the foothills. They walked northward paralleling the Lassen trail and crossing the many gullies and washes gouged out of the volcanic rock. There was little cover except scraggly greasewood to support game, and the hunters found nothing. Hardin later estimated that they had traveled northward some three or four miles when they gave up and decided to turn back. They were not sure whether they were on the east or west side of the Lassen trail. Fairfield, however, thinks it likely that they were to the east because that region was nearer to the mountains and offered the best possibilities for game.

When Hardin and Lambert crossed the lower end of a little ravine, something bright in the bottom and along its sides attracted their attention. They investigated the ravine and found a metal they took to be lead. Here was a source of bullets! They picked up 30 or 40 pounds, noting, as Hardin related later, that several wagonloads were in plain sight.

When they returned to camp, the two men found that the ore melted easily, and they made some bullets. Hardin kept a small piece and threw the rest away at the campsite. Many versions of the story claim that everyone with the train saw the ore, agreed that it was silver, and concurred in the opinion that there was enough in the ravine to make them all rich. One version, however, maintains that none of the party knew the value of the find. Hardin, that story says, tried to induce one of the men to haul the ore, but the man declared that he would not take it even if he knew it was gold.

In the light of what happened later, it would seem that nobody, including Hardin and Lambert, had any idea of what that ore was worth.

One account has it that when Hardin reached Shasta City in northern California, he showed a piece of the ore to the local miners and they saw at once that it was silver. They were not interested, however, in where it came from nor how much of it there was. It was gold they were looking for, but even gold would not lure them into the Black Rock country. There is little on which to base this unrealistic version of the story. Apparently, the piece of ore kept by Hardin arrived in Petaluma, California, where he settled down as a blacksmith, wheelwright and carpenter. Various people saw the piece of ore, and about 1857 it is said to have fallen into the hands of an assayer who found that it was carbonate of lead and silver and very rich in silver.

About this time Hardin met A. B. Jenison (often misspelled Jamison) and Frederick Alberding. They were newly arrived from the Rogue River section of Oregon. When they heard the story of the silver from Hardin, Alberding was quite amazed. He had been told exactly the same story by a man in Oregon who claimed to have been one of the original discoverers of the silver. This man could have been no one but John Lambert.

Whether or not Alberding urged Hardin to organize an expedition to search for the silver is not clear. But on July 9, 1859, the Petaluma *Journal* reported: "A party of 15 or 18 men left this locality a few days ago for the eastern slope of the Sierra Nevadas, where they go in search of what they believe to be an immense deposit of silver ore." The item added that Hardin was the leader of the group and that they intended to be gone about two months.

When Hardin and his followers arrived at Double Hot Springs, he was certain that he would have no trouble locating the ravine where, ten years earlier, he had seen silver ore by the wagonload. But the search stretched on into the fall and ended a complete failure. Finally giving up in disgust, the party started back to California.

When the weary, disappointed searchers reached Honey Lake Valley, California, they learned that a party of Honey Lakers had recently set out for the Black Rock country. They were followed three days later by another party of three men, including Lemericus Wyatt, Edward Clapper and Peter Lassen, for whom the Lassen Cutoff had been named. Both parties were in search of the lost silver and had agreed to rendezvous at Double Hot Springs.

The Lassen party arrived at the springs first and made camp at the mouth of a ravine along a small stream now known as Clapper Creek. On the following morning when the other party did not appear, Edward Clapper set out to find them. Later in the day, he gave up and returned to camp. Then he and Lassen found footprints and tracks of shod horses in the sand. They assumed that they had missed their friends and that the men were camped somewhere up the mountain.

That evening a mounted Indian mysteriously circled the Lassen camp, appearing first from one direction and then from another. Lassen coaxed the man into the camp and conversed with him in Paiute. As they talked, they heard the sound of a distant gunshot, and the Indian exclaimed, "Pai-u-tah!" He then explained that six of his tribesmen were nearby. That night, the three white men went to sleep thinking they were safe in Paiute country.

But at daybreak, there was a sudden fusillade of shots from a neighboring bluff. Lassen and Wyatt leaped up and began collecting their gear. When they tried to arouse Clapper, they found that he had been shot through the head. Lassen seized his rifle just as there was another volley, and he too was dead. Wyatt dashed for the horses. They had pulled their pickets and stampeded. He finally caught them and made his escape to Honey Lake Valley.

The other party had reached Black Rock two days before and had camped about a mile from the murder scene. Unaware of what happened, they prospected as long as their food lasted and then left for home. On the way out, they met a search party headed by Wyatt. It was their first news of their companions' fate. The mystery of Lassen's and Clapper's deaths has never been explained. There was considerable feeling at the time that they had been killed not by Paiutes but by other white men who feared they were getting too close to the Black Rock ledge.

In the spring of 1860, Hardin was back in the Black Rock country with another group from Petaluma. They were joined by most of those from the first search party who had spent the winter in Honey Lake Valley. Again they searched throughout the summer and late into the fall, but they had no more success than before, and the party disbanded in disgust.

There is reason to believe that Hardin renewed the search a third time with about 80 men, but the date is uncertain. The historian, Thompson, who accompanied this large expedition, says nothing about Hardin being along.

During the next few years the Honey Lakers kept up an almost constant search for the Hardin silver. In the early part of 1866, some of them discovered a ledge they thought to be the lost Hardin lode. The news spread, and men poured into the Black Rock country from California and other parts of Nevada. Hardin himself seems not to have been among them.

The excitement of 1866 brought conflicting claims as to the value of the ledge where Hardin is believed to have made his original find. Assays from one source showed rich ore, while the same ore assayed by another source was reported to be worthless. Nevertheless, the area seemed promising enough to the Evans brothers to establish a mill at a place five or six miles north of Double Hot Springs that came to be known as Hardin City.

The place was described by the Washoe City *Eastern Slope* as "a city of 15 houses and 15,000 rats." Other mills were built at Double Hot Springs, at Granite, and at Black Rock.

When it was learned that a sample of the Black Rock ore resembled an ore found in Freiberg, Germany, a sample was sent there to a chemist named Charles Isenbeck. Isenbeck reported that the ore was fabulously rich in silver, but could be worked only with a milling process which he had developed. One of the milling companies hired the German to install his process at a reported salary of $1,000 a month. He held the position for two years without one single accomplishment.

In 1869, Raymond W. Rossiter, United States Special Commissioner of Mining Statistics, revealed the true nature of the fraud perpetrated by Isenbeck. His process had called for the use of a secret flux which, of course, included a silver compound that showed worthless ore to have a value of from $70 to $400 per ton. On such results his employers had built a mill and placed him in charge of it. Isenbeck, of course, could not afford to use the silver compound on a large scale. When the mill was completed he simply disappeared.

A. B. Jenison, one of Hardin's original partners in the Black Rock search, prospected the region until 1884. Others did not give up until 1900.

No one found anything of value. By 1886, Hardin City had been abandoned to become a ghost town.

William H. (Billy) Jenison, son of A. B., was reared in the Black Rock country, knew the area well, and was familiar with the silver ore Hardin had found there. In April of 1909 when mining excitement was high all over Nevada, he decided to have another look at the region in which Hardin had made his find.

When he arrived at the wreckage that marked the site of Hardin City, he found that other prospectors had already been there that spring. From all appearances they had left the vicinity about a month before his arrival and had thrown their combined ore specimens on the ground in a pile. He examined this pile of discarded specimens and found a piece of ore that was exactly like that gathered by Hardin and Lambert in 1849. So far as it is known it was the first piece of this ore seen by anyone since that time. It may have been picked up at the original ledge by a prospector who did not know what it was. It may have been a piece of float picked up miles away from the ledge, or it may have been a piece of ore left by Allen Hardin at the Double Hot Springs campsite in 1849.

There have been many explanations about the value of the ore taken out of the Black Rock country. But the one offered by Fairfield seems to be the most logical. He declared that most of the ore from the Black Rock region was worked in the same mills handling the fabulously rich Comstock silver ore. The batteries and pans of these mills were not thoroughly cleaned of the Comstock ore when the poorer, or worthless, Black Rock ore was processed. Some of the high quality material must have been mixed with the Black Rock ore. Invariably, the Black Rock ore, when processed by itself, showed a poor assay.

The Black Rock country is subject to frequent cloudbursts during the hot summer months. Men who knew the country well in the sixties and returned there 25 years later reported that it did not look like the same terrain. New canyons had been carved out and old ones filled in by the flow of water. It was Fairfield's opinion that two or three years before Hardin first visited the region, a violent storm had torn open the side of a hill and exposed the rich ledge which Hardin and Lambert stumbled upon. Before Hardin returned to the place, another cloudburst had covered it up. This view was shared by several prospectors with whom Fairfield discussed his theory. If this is the case, who knows but that the next cloudburst may again expose the ledge to view? But it may also remain buried forever.

Humboldt County— The news that Allen Hardin was leading a party into the Black Rock country in search of the silver ledge he had found ten years previously received widespread publicity and aroused great interest. Several parties decided to beat him to it. Among these was Henry Comstock and his partners who were mining unprofitably at Gold Canyon near Virginia City.

NEVADA

Deserting their efforts in Gold Canyon, Comstock and five men started for the Black Rock Range. Comstock's motives in this venture were very suspect. Many people believed that if he found the Hardin ledge, he intended to take some of the ore, pack it back to Gold Canyon, salt the claims he had cheated other prospectors out of, and sell them to unsuspecting San Francisco promoters.

Comstock's party apparently arrived in the Black Rock country well ahead of Hardin's party and immediately found a ledge of silver. After taking out all the ore they could pack, they covered the ledge with rock and gravel to conceal it from the Hardin party. In the summer of 1859, after the Black Rock excitement subsided, Comstock announced the discovery of silver at Gold Canyon. His scheme had worked. He sold his claims for $40,000! Losing interest now in mining, he drifted away and later appeared in Idaho where he died bankrupt.

Whether or not the Comstock group actually found the Lost Hardin Mine is a matter of conjecture. Some people claim that he made an entirely new discovery. Others believe that he made no discovery at all. Among the few things that history can definitely record about Henry Comstock is that he was completely unreliable and unscrupulous.

Humboldt County—J. M. Hunter worked in the mines around Sonoma in 1850. In 1881, when he was living in Santa Barbara, California, he gave the following account of gold in the Sierras to the Nevada historian, Myron Angel:

In the mining camps around Sonoma there were always stories of rich diggings on the eastern slopes of the Sierras. These stories were carried to California by emigrants passing through Carson Valley. Many reported that they had been shown large nuggets of gold by Mormon settlers and told that the gold had been found in the hills to the north where it existed in large quantities

When asked why they had not stopped to mine this gold, the emigrants had a standard reply. They were short of provisions, and it was impossible to winter in Carson Valley. They, therefore, had to move on westward. But many resolved to return and search for the Mormon gold if they did not find wealth in California.

A party of some fifty Californians did, indeed, return to Nevada in 1850 and prospected the region from the Walker River south to Devil's Gate, a defile on the Gold Canyon Road between Virginia City and Silver City. Here they spent almost a month. They found gold but not in quantity. Whether or not this was the gold referred to by the emigrants has never been determined.

Humboldt County—During the gold rush days, a wagon train was returning east from California. Its members had been successful in the California mines and their wagons carried much gold. On the journey they met an Indian who was in need and gave him food and clothing. Out of gratitude the redman attached himself to the party as a kind of self-appointed advance guard and scout. In this country where a friendly Indian was rare, his services were welcome.

Riding ahead one day in his chosen position, the Indian met some tribesmen on the warpath. Unable to turn them back by persuasion, he eluded them and raced back to warn the white men whom he found camped at the base of a mountain peak in the northern part of what is now Humboldt County.

When the travelers heard the Indian's warning, they quickly unloaded their gold and buried it on the slope of the peak and prepared to defend themselves against the impending attack. At dawn the following day, they were overwhelmed by screaming redskins. All members of the wagon train were killed. Their wagons were rifled and burned.

It is said that a man named Thompson, the first surveyor in that part of the country, found the remains of the wagons years later and named the cliff Disaster Peak. The Disaster Peak Treasure has never been found.

Humboldt County—Little is known of an old, white-bearded prospector named Old Man Berry, or sometimes affectionately called "Uncle Berry."

One time Berry was camped at Black Rock Point, a noted landmark at the southern extremity of the Black Rock Range. He picked up a large gold nugget lying at the edge of the road where it skirted the foothills. He knew that the gold was either float broken from its ledge and left there by the forces of nature or dropped by some traveler. Though his provisions were running low, and he was in dangerous Indian country, he delayed his journey as long as he could to search the nearby foothills for a ledge. He found nothing and continued on his way to California.

Sometime later he heard about a Frenchman's find which renewed his interest in his piece of float. Many years before, a Frenchman who lived in Sacramento was traveling eastward along the Old Emigrant Trail. About 40 miles east of the California-Nevada line, a sudden storm forced him to seek shelter in a cave. The day was bitterly cold. He gathered some dried sagebrush stumps and built a fire. As the flames roared up and flooded the cave with light, he saw scattered on the floor large nuggets of gold. Others were embedded in the soft walls and he could pry them out with his knife. At the rear, the cave narrowed to a slit. Taking a firebrand, he held it into the slit as far as possible and was able to see that the opening again widened and that the floor there too was covered with gold.

Gathering all the gold he could carry in a flour sack, he tied it to the pommel of his saddle and rode eastward. The jogging motion of the horse wore a hole in the sack and slowly released a trail of gold nuggets. When the Frenchman discovered his loss, he retraced his steps for some distance, trying to recover the nuggets, but he was unable to find many of them. Tying the rest of the nuggets tightly together in the sack so that they would not spill out again, he resumed his journey.

Eventually, he returned to Sacramento and told of his experience in the cave.

When Berry heard the story, he felt certain that the nugget he had picked up along the road west of the Black Rock Range was one of those dropped by the Frenchman. He is said to have spent the rest of his life seeking the Frenchman's Lost Cave of Gold.

Humboldt County—In the early days of the west, Job Taylor kept a trading post in Indian Valley in northeastern California, near the Nevada border. His place was much frequented by the Indians of the region, and it was not unusual for them to trade gold nuggets for the things they required. One day a brave brought in gold nuggets of extraordinary size and richness. Taylor questioned him as to where they had come from. The Indian, of course, refused to answer.

Later, he returned with more of the large nuggets, and again Taylor was unsuccessful in securing any information from him. After a year or more, however, the white man gained the redman's confidence. The Indian agreed to tell all he knew of the place where the gold was located in exchange for a large amount of merchandise, and for still more merchandise he promised to lead Taylor to the gold. Taylor induced a Captain Wetherell to join him, and the three set out eastward for the creek the Indian said was filled with the nuggets.

They camped at a spot near Granite Creek Mountain and near which Chief Winnemucca was encamped with his people. The Indian guide said he had a message for the Paiute chief and departed with instructions for the white men to wait. He returned the next day and repudiated his agreement with Taylor, saying that the chief had threatened to have him killed if he revealed where the gold was. No inducement could change the Indian's mind and the search had to be abandoned. Taylor and Wetherell returned to California. The Indian was never seen again at Taylor's trading post.

The following year, however, an Indian boy appeared at the post with large nuggets which Taylor recognized as the same kind the brave had traded. When questioned, the boy talked freely, but denied that he had ever seen the place the gold came from. He declared that the nuggets had been given to him by his elders who had never allowed him to know where they got them. But he had overheard enough talk, he said, to believe that he could find the place.

Nevertheless, he stubbornly refused all inducements Taylor and Wetherell offered him to lead them to the gold. Finally he did agree to take them to an old man who lived near the place where the two men had camped at Granite Mountain. The old Indian was an outcast from the tribe, and the boy thought he might tell where the gold was.

Following the same trail Taylor and Wetherell had taken previously, the boy led them to the outcast Indian. But the old man denied any knowledge of the gold. The two white men took the boy aside and frightened him with threats. The boy then agreed to take them to the gold, but at the end of the first day's travel he disappeared from their camp. Taylor made frequent searches afterward, but the secret of the Indian mine eluded him—and all others.

The riches Taylor and Wetherell sought might possibly be in a canyon near Eblings in Virginia Valley, where the Indians once mined for gold. Many people believe this canyon is the place where a party of west-bound emigrants found the famous "Blue Bucket" gold. Strong evidence, however, suggests that The Lost Blue Bucket Mine is in Oregon.

Humboldt County—Buffalo Springs are along Buffalo Creek south of the small town of Orovada. There is a story of unknown origin about a Spanish padre who traveled through this country long before the arrival of the white man. The priest, tradition says, worked a rich gold mine near Buffalo Springs. When he became ill, his workmen closed the mine and took him to Mexico where he died.

But the padre had recorded the event in his journal and prepared a map describing the location of his mine. It is said that this map was discovered by a Californian searching through old records in Mexico City. He organized a party and made an extensive search for the mine, but it was never found. The party, however, came upon two gold nuggets in the region described on the map, and this strengthened the belief that the mine actually existed. Today even the map is lost.

Lander County—Hickison Summit is crossed by US 50 east of Austin. The story is told that two miners returning east from California with a considerable quantity of gold reached this spot when an argument arose over the division of their jointly acquired riches. One man, without the knowledge of the other, buried the gold where they camped that night.

The next morning, their argument ended in a gun duel. The man who had buried the gold was killed, and his partner was never able to find it. Returning east alone, he later told friends that their camp had been made at a place called The Peaks, a name unknown to natives in the area. The gold has not yet been unearthed.

Lincoln County—This is a story told by old residents, and like most of its kind, the facts simply cannot be traced to their source. Yet many people have searched the ruins of Delamar with spades and metal detectors for a treasure they apparently believe to be there.

Delamar, jammed halfway up a shallow rocky canyon, was once one of the largest and best gold-producing camps in southeastern Nevada. By 1906, its mines had produced an official $25,000,000. But Delamar was also a dangerous mine for its laborers. About three months in the mines there were enough for a miner to contract fatal silicosis. A few years after 1906, the mines had come to a complete halt, and people were hastily moving away.

NEVADA

During Delamar's heyday one mill alone shipped out from $100,000 to $200,000 worth of bullion in an ordinary freight wagon without a guard, a guise designed to thwart robbers. Apparently the ruse worked, but there was a theft from another source.

According to stories told by those who knew the camp in its early days, an unnamed mine official of the Jackrabbit Mine, working in collusion with an assayer, managed to accumulate $70,000 worth of stolen bullion which he buried until the time when he thought he could safely smuggle it out of the camp. But that day never came. The speculator died before he could carry out his plan. It is said that he never told the assayer where the bullion was hidden.

Although Delamar is essentially a ghost town, a few hardy people still live there with the hope that the mines will one day come back. Some also live in the hope of finding the Jackrabbit Mine official's lost treasure.

Lincoln County—In the summer of 1867, Sam Vail and Robert Knox made camp in Pahranagat Valley about 10 miles below Hiko. They were driving a herd of several hundred half-broken wild mustangs they had gathered in central Nevada and were taking north to sell in the Mormon farming settlements of Utah. Natives of the valley thought it quite strange that the visitors, instead of moving on in a few days, stayed several months. It was noted also that their herd seemed to increase and decrease mysteriously. All questions asked of the strangers were evaded.

In late summer, the camp was suddenly abandoned and a party of Paiute Indians reported finding a half-buried saddle at the campsite. It bore the initials RK burned into the leather.

Officials went to the site and dug up the body of Robert Knox. A coroner's inquest found that he had been killed by an axe blow on the head. The officers returned an indictment against his missing partner, Sam Vail. The motive for the murder was established as Vail's efforts to secure the horses for himself, their accumulated cash, and a $3,000 cashier's check belonging to Knox drawn on the Bank of California. The prolonged search for Vail resulted in his capture near Austin. He was returned to Hiko, tried, convicted and hanged.

In the last hour of his life, Vail wrote a letter to the sister of the murdered Knox in which he confessed the crime. He also revealed that he had secured Knox's cashier's check and the $15,000 they had accumulated from their joint horse-trading. These, he stated, he had placed in a fruit jar and buried near the spot where Knox's body had been found. The site had been marked with a large wooden stake. Vail wanted the sister to have the money so that she could give her brother a decent burial.

Not until Knox's sister had visited the campsite several times did she reveal the contents of Vail's letter. She failed to find the treasure, as did many others who searched later.

TREASURE GUIDE

Lincoln County—About 1860, a Paiute Indian came into a prospector's camp somewhere in southeastern Lincoln County with exceedingly rich gold ore which he wished to exchange for some fancied article possessed by the white man. Not satisfied with trading for the ore at hand, the prospector determined to find out where it had come from. After a long and solemn discussion with much bickering, it developed that the Indian passionately desired the white man's bridle. Finally, the deal was made. In exchange for the bridle, the Indian agreed to lead the prospector to the body of ore.

After a short journey, the two men arrived at a secluded spot and the Indian, true to his word, pointed out the ore. Upon examination, the ore proved to be heavily-impregnated with gold. To the Indian's great surprise, the white man now demanded the return of the bridle. The Indian angrily refused and a fight ensued. The redman was wounded and fled. After picking up all the ore samples he could carry, the prospector took his reclaimed bridle and left. He realized that the wounded Indian would soon return with his vengeful people.

Luckily, the prospector met a company of soldiers on a scouting expedition from their camp at Reveille. But it was not long before a party of Indians overtook the soldiers and recognized the swindling prospector. When they demanded that he be surrendered to them for punishment, a fight resulted and the Indians dispersed after several of them were killed.

The prospector knew that he would never dare to return to the ore as long as there were Paiutes in the vincinity, nor could he seek aid for fear of revealing his act of treachery.

Years later, when he was about to die, he called in a friend, gave him specimens of the ore which he had carefully preserved, and produced a crude map he had drawn of the region. The friend and others believed the map described a place near Quartz Peak in the northern section of the Pint Water Range, but they were never able to decipher the prospector's chart. The district is now in the Nellis Air Force Range and Nuclear Testing Site.

Mineral County—In 1908, a prospector named Tim Cody gave up his part-time mining job to prospect in the area around Cedar Mountain. Cedar Mountain was almost on the Mineral-Esmeralda County line. One day he left his base camp at Stewart Springs northeast of Mina to walk the 15 miles to the mining camp of Golddyke, still farther to the northeast. It was no distance for a prospector, and he took with him only enough food and water for the few hour's trip. Somewhere along the route, Tim lost his way in the featureless bed of an ancient dried-up lake and wandered until late evening. In search of a landmark, he climbed a small juniper-covered knoll for a better view of the surrounding country. To the north, he recognized Paradise Peak and was able to orient himself.

Relieved that he would not have to spend the night on the desert, Cody sat down for a rest before resuming his journey. The white, iron-stained

NEVADA

quartz at his feet would attract the attention of any informed prospector, and Tim knew gold signs when he saw them. He examined a piece and then another and another. They were the same. In the growing dusk he could not determine the extent of the ledge, but what he saw was enough to excite him. He marked some of the nearby junipers so that he would have no trouble in relocating the spot. Then picking up all the ore he could carry, he hurried on toward Golddyke.

It was perhaps the excitement that caused him to lose his way the second time. He wandered through the night, the next day, and the next. But at the end of the following day he came to an old abandoned mine he knew. It was ten miles from his camp at Stewart Springs. He was out of both food and water. But by a stroke of fortune, someone had cached supplies in the old mine shaft, and Tim Cody was spared the fate he had feared.

As soon as he felt revived, he set out again and this time reached Golddyke. When his business was completed there, he left for his camp, intending to locate and survey the little juniper-covered knoll on his way.

He did not miss his trail on the return trip, nor did he locate the knoll. There were many knolls and they all looked alike, but not one revealed the blazed junipers. Cody carried on his search for a full year without success. He lived until 1930, still hoping to find the desert knoll rich with gold.

Mineral County—When Belleville was a booming mining camp, an employee of one of the big mills there stole a considerable number of iron flasks filled with quicksilver (mercury). Each of these flasks weighed 76 pounds, and its value at that time was about $40. Such bulky items could hardly be hidden around a cabin or transported inconspicuously. Authorities assumed that the flasks were probably concealed in a dry well or prospect hole to lie there until the thief thought they were forgotten.

He eventually moved away, and it was believed that he was never able to get the flasks out of Belleville. This theory was proved correct when, years later, the thief's son came to Belleville and tried to find the flasks. His father had passed the secret on to him. By then old Belleville was almost deserted. The son searched every conceivable foot of the empty village and dug in every likely spot, but he failed to locate his father's loot.

Even today, when the price of mercury rises, there are those who still search for Belleville's hidden quicksilver.

Nye County—In 1871, a French Canadian prospector known only as Duckett left the mining camp of Belmont on horseback with a second horse carrying his pack. He headed toward the Colorado River and was near Pillar Springs when he found himself running out of water. In his search for it, he climbed a small juniper-covered hill where he came face to face with a Paiute Indian. Through signs he made the Indian understand that he was looking for water, and the redman led him along a faint trail to a large ravine. A short distance down the ravine they came to a spring of

31

water.

After Duckett had replenished his supply of water and given his horses a chance to drink, he asked the Indian, again in sign language, if he knew of any gold. After some hesitation, the Indian produced samples of ore he had with him and showed them to the prospector. Duckett could see that the gold content of the rock was high, but the Indian remained silent as to its source. After prolonged dickering, the Indian agreed to take Duckett to the ore in exchange for one of his horses. The deal was made and they rode away together.

About three miles farther on, the Indian pointed to an outcropping and quickly rode away. Duckett gathered several pounds of the ore and decided to return to the spring to make camp before other Indians learned of his presence.

The next morning he left for Belmont. Before traveling far, he spotted two Indians on his trail. They soon overtook him and demanded his horse. In a short fight, Duckett killed both Indians and fled. The ore he had taken assayed $15,000 to the ton.

Afraid to enter the Indian country again, Duckett waited three years in the hope that the killing of the two Indians would by that time be forgotten. In 1874, he and two companions rode south from Hamilton, intending to approach Pillar Springs from the east. A short distance west of Hiko they were stopped by a party of Paiutes and warned to turn back. Being outnumbered and faced with a group that showed every intention of keeping white men out of their territory, the prospectors left.

Duckett is said to have made several attempts later to find the outcropping, but he always failed. Eventually, he was attracted to the great strike at Cripple Creek, Colorado, and dropped from sight. He reportedly left a map of the area with a man in Ely, Nevada, and from this map others tried to locate the lost outcropping. If the ore is close to Pillar Springs, it is on the Nellis Air Force Range and Nuclear Testing Site.

Nye County—The remains of the old mining camp of Tybo can still be found on some modern maps though it has almost completely vanished as an active community. It is west of US 6 directly north of Warm Springs. During the hectic mining days, Tybo and the nearby camp of Belmont were connected by daily stagecoaches.

The story is told of a Belmont gambler who regularly took the stage to Tybo on paydays to fleece the miners in a crooked game. One day when he left Tybo to return to Belmont, he was carrying $3,000 in winnings in a leather sack. At McCann's Summit, a few miles north of Tybo, the gambler requested the driver to stop the stage. Supposing the man had to answer a call to nature, the driver stopped. Carrying his sack of money, the gambler got off the stage and asked the driver to go down the road a mile and wait for him. Again the driver obliged. When the gambler returned to the stage, he was not carrying his sack of money. He remarked to the driver that he would return for it later when things cooled off. Three days afterward, he was killed in a card game argument in Belmont. It is believed that his $3,000 were never recovered.

Nye County—Another treasure believed to be buried near Tybo belonged to a man who operated the nearby charcoal kilns. Like many others of his day, he did not trust banks. He put his money in the ground. One day, he received a $5,000 payment for charcoal delivered to a smelter. This money he is supposed to have buried near the Tybo charcoal kilns. A few days later, when the charcoal operator failed to appear at the kilns, a party went out in search of him. His body was found with a broken neck. Apparently, he had been thrown from his horse. His money is possibly still buried near the old kilns.

Nye County—Jack Allen was disgusted with his luck as a miner and prospector in California. He decided to try the new mining camps in Nevada. Crossing Death Valley, he turned north, skirted the western edge of Pahute Mesa, traveled to the east of the Stonewall Mountains, and arrived at the southern base of Mount Helen. While making his way through a canyon, he picked up a piece of quartz that showed promising color. He gathered all he could carry and headed for the nearest settlement, noting carefully the landmarks along the way so that he could return to the site.

When his ore assayed $32,000 to the ton, he outfitted himself and returned to the canyon to put up his monument and claim notices. Although he had been away from the spot only a few days, he could not locate one single landmark that remained so vividly in his mind. Then it occurred to him that the entire terrain had been changed by a devastating cloudburst. Disgusted now with Nevada, he returned to California. The site of Jack Allen's lost ledge is in the Nellis Air Force Range and Nuclear Testing Site.

Nye County—A local story tells of a freighter who was caught in a furious sandstorm about seven miles south of Beatty. He turned his horses loose to fend for themselves until the storm abated and bedded himself down under his wagon which was loaded with whiskey. When the gale blew over, the horses had disappeared and the freighter had to walk into Beatty. Days later when he returned to the scene, the wagon had competely vanished, presumably covered by another sandstorm.

In spite of many searches, nobody has ever admitted to having found the wagon with its treasure of aged whiskey.

Nye County—There is a story that a man known only as Sam buried a gallon jar of gold nuggets on his property near the almost deserted town of Manhattan. It is also said that Sam buried a metal pipe filled with silver dollars on that property. His wealth was estimated at $80,000. His property consisted of three houses in a row at the edge of town joined by several empty lots to the west. Although the houses are now gone, it is said that old residents of Manhattan can point out their sites.

Sam once remarked that he could see the place where his money was buried when he sat on his front porch. Some Manhattanites say this would have placed the treasure on one of his lots. Others contend that his wealth was buried on a line with the old mill to the west, which is now in ruins. Residents of the languishing village believe that Sam's treasure is still there.

Nye County—About 1875, two characters who enlivened Hiko with their presence were known as Tempiute Bill and Moquitch. They were suspected of a number of robberies and possibly a few murders.

A miner at Crescent Wash was found brutally beaten to death with a rock, and all evidence pointed to Tempiute Bill and Moquitch as the criminals. When the two partners learned that the vigilantes were about to strike, they suddenly vanished into the desert and mountain ranges of Nye County. After eluding Sheriff Bidwell's posse for more than five months, the criminals were captured and brought back to Hiko. They were met at the edge of town by a delegation bent on holding an immediate necktie party. But Sheriff Bidwell convinced the crowd that, since he had chased down the criminals, he should be allowed to participate in the legal hanging after the trial. The trial, he assured them, would be fair and legal, but it was clear that the verdict had already been pronounced.

Tempiute Bill and Moquitch admitted the killing of the Crescent Wash miner because he had refused to reveal where his cache of gold was hidden. They implicated a man known only as Johnny, and the vigilantes rode out to his camp intent upon placing his neck in their noose. Johnny saw them coming and elected to shoot it out rather than stretch the rope. He was killed. Tempiute Bill and Moquitch were duly tried, found guilty and immediately hanged.

What happened to the dead miner's cache of gold? No one had the answer, but many searched for it.

In the days before people had faith in banks, most miners knew only two courses of action to take with their wealth—either spend it or bury it. Seldom did anyone but the owner know where his money was buried. When he died, his gold remained where it was hidden, unless someone stumbled upon it by accident.

Nye County—About 1890, two unnamed prospectors began to investigate a mountain near Tonopah for mineral specimens. One side of the mountain was a precipitous and insurmountable cliff. The other side was less formidable, and the prospectors were able to climb it. From the top of the cliff they looked down and saw a narrow ledge about 500 feet below. Working their way down over a rough trail, they found themselves perched on an overhanging ledge of greater width than they had judged it to be from above. In the rock on the side of the mountain they discovered a rich vein of gold.

NEVADA

During the weeks that followed, the two men laboriously carried one log at a time down the dangerous trail and built a crude cabin on the ledge. It was precariously perched there, but it offered shelter and practical invisibility from prying eyes. Although work on the mine was impossible after the first heavy snowfall, the miners did not leave their hut until it was clear they could survive there no longer. They started down the mountain and plunged 2,500 feet to their death. When their bodies were discovered the following spring, a search was made for their mine, but the trail down to it and the cabin on the ledge had been completely obliterated by landslides. The only evidence of the existence of their cabin and ledge of gold came from the miners' own story confided to a friend who did not divulge it until after the prospectors' bodies were found.

Ormsby (Carson City) County—Sometimes in the early days of Nevada, a date variously given from 1870 to 1890, a stagecoach left Virginia City for the mint in Carson City carrying $60,000 worth of gold bullion. Highway men were so common in that day and region that extra guards were added to protect the strongbox.

The stagecoach was approaching Carson City when four men appeared brandishing weapons and brought the stage to a screeching halt. With the precision and dispatch typical of men experienced in their trade, the bandits secured the strongbox and waved the stage on.

One version of the story says that the four men made their escape and were later snared by a posse. Three were killed, and the fourth, a Mexican, was captured. Another version has it that the guards collected their wits and fired upon the men, killing two of them.

In any case, the story goes that the bandits found the strongbox too heavy to carry and buried it somewhere in the sage-covered hills northeast of Carson City. The lone survivor was convicted and sentenced to a term in the Nevada State Prison which stood on the southeastern outskirts of Carson City. According to the story, he asked for and was given a cell which looked out over the open country toward the spot where the loot was supposedly hidden. Throughout his imprisonment, he refused to reveal where the $60,000 were concealed.

After serving eight years of his term, Wells Fargo, which had been entrusted with the bullion, influenced the government to grant the prisoner full pardon. Apparently, the company hoped that the freed man would lead them to the stolen gold. The released prisoner, however, was in the last stages of tuberculosis and unable to recover the loot.

A German butcher befriended the Mexican and, seeing that the man had but a short time to live, tried to learn the secret hiding place of the gold from him. The ailing man finally agreed to lead the butcher and his son to the treasure site. As the Mexican was about to mount his horse for the trip into the sagebrush hills, he fell dead.

Some persons maintain that the warden of the State Prison in 1935 considered suggestions that convicts be allowed to search for the treasure, but no action was taken. Matt R. Penrose, who was at one time Superintendent of Nevada State Police and Warden of Nevada State Penitentiary, tells the story of the Carson City gold in his book, "Pots O'Gold", but he fails to offer any documentation.

Pershing County—In the early 1900's, Peter Prengle and a friend left Lovelock to prospect in the Humboldt Range. They made camp one night at a spot about seven miles north of Antelope Springs and awoke in the morning to find that their burros had strayed away. While his partner prepared to break camp, Prengle went in search of the animals. Climbing to the crest of a high pass, he stopped to examine a ledge and found it to be rich in gold.

He piled up a small monument of rocks to mark the spot, rounded up the burros, and returned to the camp. The trip was apparently fruitless, since Prengle did not reveal his find to his partner. They looked around a little more and then returned to Lovelock.

At the first opportunity, Prengle slipped off alone and went back to the site of his find. But he was never able to locate the pile of rocks he had built.

Pershing County—During emigrant days, lush wild grasses grew in the bed of Humboldt Sink. West-bound wagon trains stopped there to fatten their stock, soak their shrunken wagon wheels, and rest before plunging into the sand and heat of the dreaded Forty-Mile Desert to the southwest. Today, the Sink is nothing more than barren clay bottoms through which the Humboldt River finds its way. It straddles the Pershing-Churchill County

One day in 1909, two young men stepped off the eastbound stage at Humboldt, a small settlement near the famed Sink. Without tarrying or revealing any of their plans, they walked into a general store, outfitted themselves and purchased a week's supply of food. With their equipment and supplies packed on their backs, they left town in a westerly direction.

Two weeks later, the two young men walked back into Humboldt and inquired when the next stage left for the west. Told that it would be the following day, they sat down in the store to rest. L. W. Morgan introduced himself to them and asked if they had had any luck. One of the men handed him a piece of ore. Morgan assumed that it was silver, but it was unlike any he had ever seen in Nevada. The young men told him this story:

During the rush to the gold fields, their grandfather had joined a California-bound wagon train. When the group arrived at the edge of the Humboldt Sink, as was customary, they stopped to let the stock rest and graze. The grandfather took his gun and went in search of fresh meat. He started eastward and returned after several hours without game. But he did bring back a few pounds of what he took to be lead ore and tossed it into a bucket in the back of the wagon.

NEVADA

He carried the ore samples all the way to San Francisco, where the largest piece was used as a door stop for many years. One day a mining man visiting in the grandfather's home saw the ore and asked to have it assayed. It showed high values in lead and silver.

The grandfather never went back for the ore, but when he died, he left documents relating to the discovery and directions to its location. These had come into the possession of his two grandsons.

And how did the young men come by the piece of ore they showed Morgan? During their search, they said, they had found nothing and were about to give up when they came upon an old deserted camp. Tools and cooking utensils were scattered around and there were signs that a tent had once been there. On the spot where they guessed the tent had stood, they had discovered the piece of ore. Morgan, an experienced miner, assured the young men that the ore could not be float so it had to be carried there by someone.

On the following day, the young men boarded the stage for San Francisco. Apparently they never tried again to find the ore discovered by their grandfather.

Storey County—Somewhere in the rugged country northwest of Virginia City, legend says that a man-made arch of stones once marked a cache of gold stolen from Virginia City. Though several parties have searched diligently for the treasure, neither the arch nor the gold has been found. The arch, about five feet high, is said to have been seen by persons unaware of the treasure it was supposed to indicate. Since then, it is believed that the arch has fallen. No one seems to know the details of the theft nor when it happened.

Storey County—James Fennimore was known as Old Virginny because he came from Virginia and never let anyone forget it. He had come west with the horde of Forty-Niners and drifted into Nevada from California. In 1858, he found an outcropping of gold on Sun Mountain, which is now called Mount Davidson. Putting up a location marker and writing out a claim of notice, which was enough to comply with the mining laws in those days, he placed the notice under a rock, got drunk, and promptly forgot it.

From time to time, Old Virginny took out enough gold to keep him in booze, but nothing more. When large mining interests arrived at the Comstock, they began buying up all claims. Old Virginny sold his claim for a bottle of whiskey and a leather bag containing $7,500 in gold coins. The deal took place in a mine shaft. By the time Virginny finished the bottle and was ready to start back to Virginia City, he was drunk and afraid to carry the gold coins with him. Emerging from the mine, he slipped the bag of gold under a rock, staggered away, and could never remember under which rock he had hidden his coins. He had lost his gold and traded a mining claim that made its new owners millions.

TREASURE GUIDE

Considering the thousands of prospectors and miners who trod the area in later years, it would be a miracle if Old Virginny's bag of gold has not been found.

Storey County—There is no question that Allen and Hosea Grosch found a vein of silver ore near Mount Davidson, but it is quite possible that this vein was later rediscovered during the great Comstock excitement. It seems improbable that any ore of value could have been overlooked in the intensive search made of the region at that time when it was easily accessible to thousands of prospectors. There is, however, always an element of doubt, and no one can be sure that the Grosch vein was discovered. The only three men who ever saw it died without passing on any exact information as to its location.

Ethan Allen Grosch and Hosea Ballou Grosch were sons of a Pennsylvania minister and editor of some note. Both had been well educated in chemistry and mineralogy. Both were stable and respected. In 1849, they sailed from Philadelphia to Tampico, Mexico, and traveled overland to Mazatlan where they boarded a vessel for California. It was an ill-starred trip. Hosea became very ill, and in the Pacific their ship barely survived a storm.

It was the summer of 1850 before the Grosch brothers reached the California gold fields. Their first mining venture met with little success, and in 1851 they made a prospecting trip into western Utah. On their return trip, they stopped in what later became known as Gold Canyon near present Virginia City. There they met "Old Frank," a Mexican who called their attention to the possibility of silver ore in the region. They accumulated many samples which they took back to California for testing.

The following year they returned to Gold Canyon, where there was now a little placer activity. Nothing exciting developed and they again returned to California. But, more and more convinced that Nevada offered rich silver possibilities, they were back at Gold Canyon in 1853. In the summer of 1855 they built a little cabin above Johnston camp about a mile from Virginia City. They then settled down to serious and systematic prospecting which had to be interrupted from time to time by work in the placer mines to earn enough money for provisions. They had brought with them from California a considerable library of scientific volumes, numerous assaying tools and chemical apparatus. But they seldom spoke of their investigations to the few miners with whom they rarely associated.

In the summer of 1857, the Grosch brothers were certain that they had found a rich vein of silver, and their tests proved them correct. They formed a small company, taking in mostly old friends from California. But of these only one, George Brown, a Carson Valley stockman, was shown the location of the vein. Brown agreed to finance the development of the mine when the course and extent of the vein was determined.

Another who was taken into the venture, but shown only a piece of ore from the vein, was Mrs. L. M. Dettenreider. Mrs. Dettenreider had once befriended the Grosch brothers, and they had staked out a claim for her to express their appreciation. The lady later operated a boardinghouse in Virginia City and was able to throw some light on the vein's location.

The spell of ill luck which had dogged the Grosch brothers at almost every step since they had arrived in the West seemed at last to be broken, and their early faith in the Gold Hill region appeared to be justified when an accident befell Hosea. He stuck a pick in his foot and died of gangrene two weeks later.

As soon as Allen had worked long enough to pay off the debt incurred by his brother's illness, he left Virginia City for the winter. Late in November, he and a young prospector friend from Canada, Richard M. Burke, set out for California over the Donner Summit route. It was a tragic trip. They were forced to make most of their way through waist-deep snow, but they succeeded in crawling down the western slopes of the Sierra and reaching a Mexican mining camp. The legs of both men were frozen to the knees. The Mexicans hauled them on sleds to the Last Chance mining camp where Burke had parts of both legs amputated, and he survived. Allen Grosch, however, refused amputation and died on December 19, 1857.

With the death of Allen Grosch the exact location of the silver vein was lost. Burke had seen silver from the assays and had been shown the general course of the vein on a map, but of its actual location he knew practically nothing. Mrs. Dettenreider possessed more information than anyone else, and this was meager. She said that Allen had once pointed to Mount Davidson and said, "It is down at the base of that point."

Shortly after Allen Grosch and Richard Bucke had left for California, the Grosch cabin was taken over by a lazy Canadian with the impressive name of Henry Tompkins Paige Comstock, familiarly known as "Old Pancake" because he was too indolent to make bread. He had come to Carson Valley driving a herd of sheep and preferred destitution to labor. Just how he came into possession of the Grosch cabin and its belongings will probably never be known. He told several different stories, some of them under oath. But in addition to being the laziest man in the country, he was also about the biggest liar. Once he claimed that Allen Grosch had left him in charge of the cabin until his intended return. Most people refused to accept that. A man of Allen Grosch's type would hardly select a well-known vagabond to place in charge of his books, papers and equipment for several months. On another occasion Comstock claimed that he was a partner in the mining activities of the Grosch brothers. Burke strongly denied this.

It was generally assumed that Comstock had merely appropriated the Grosch cabin to search through the brothers' papers for information as to the location of their silver ledge. This is probably near the truth. There was no secret about the Grosch discovery, and Comstock was noted for his spying on the activity of others and jumping in with claims when finds were made. The books, papers and scientific equipment disappeared from the Grosch cabin and were never found. Allen and Bucke had probably buried or hidden them before they set off on their fateful journey to California. One account has it that the assay reports and maps were secreted in a hollow pine. No proof has been presented to support any theory of what happened to the Grosch brothers' possessions.

If Comstock took the papers, he never profited from them. He later bluffed his way into part ownership of a claim which soared to a stock market quotation value of $80,000,000 — and he sold his part for $11,000 cash!

In 1860, three forgotten furnaces used by the Grosch brothers were uncovered from a deposit of mud and sand in Gold Canyon. The old furnaces renewed interest in the search for the Grosch vein. An old shaft was also discovered in a sort of sink on the mountain near the Grosch cabin. This was assumed to be the spot where the Grosch brothers had worked secretly. The place was pre-empted and called the Lost Shaft. When the pre-empters cleaned out the shaft, about the only thing they found was the body of an old Paiute squaw who had been murdered by her tribe and dumped into the hole. It was later established that the shaft had never been worked by the Grosches. It had been sunk by miners in 1851.

Many years have passed since a serious search has been made for the silver vein discovered by Allen and Hosea Grosch. Though that silver must be a part of the great Comstock Lode legend, it would be most interesting to know what secrets repose in those Grosch maps and papers.

Washoe County—On November 4, 1870, five men robbed an east-bound Central Pacific Railroad passenger train near the small station of Verdi about eight miles from Reno. A confederate had telegraphed the bandits from San Francisco that the train's express car would be carrying $60,000 in gold coins. It was a Wells Fargo shipment consigned to Reno. For his part in the crime the informant was to receive $2,895, which was to be buried at a certain spot for recovery at a later date.

The robbery succeeded. The strongbox was seized, taken into the timber, broken open, and the informant's fee counted out. The rest of the gold was divided into five parts. As agreed, the informant's $2,895 were buried near an abandoned mine tunnel overlooking the railroad at the scene of the crime. Then the bandits fled in separate directions, each hiding his share of the loot as he saw fit.

When Wells Fargo agents captured the outlaws, they all received prison sentences after revealing where their caches were hidden. All of these were recovered, but none of the robbers lived to reclaim the $2,895 buried near the little station at Verdi, and Wells Fargo agents seem never to have found it.

Washoe County—Sand Springs was an early-day stopping place on the edge of a vast desert salt deposit. Little is left of it except the filling stations that serve travelers on US 50. But in the beginning of the twentieth century, it was the locale of an unusual gold rush called "The Chicken Craw Gold Rush."

The Chicken Craw Gold Rush of 1907 started when Larry Hunt, a desert prospector, was operating a roadside inn at Sand Springs. One day he was dressing chickens for the Sunday dinner and discovered two fair-sized gold nuggets in the craws of two of the birds. He killed his entire flock and found more nuggets. Where had the chickens picked up the gold? Obviously, they had ranged over a placer deposit. But Hunt had not owned the chickens long, and he decided that they could not have eaten gold in his neighborhood.

Accompanied by a companion, he set out to learn where the chickens had come from. The man from whom he had bought them told him that he had got them in Wadsworth. Wadsworth was about fifty miles away. The previous owner there reported that he had acquired the flock from no less than four different owners in widely scattered locations. Hunt never found out where the chickens had picked up the gold.

Washoe County—Behind the Bowers Mansion, now a county museum about 20 miles from Reno, Price's Lake lies at the foot of Slide Mountain. Old residents in Carson Valley remember that the man called Price, for whom the lake was named, operated a gold mine near there. He used to bring his gold ore down the mountain, catch the train at Bowers Landing, and take it to Carson City. Before he died, he covered all traces of his mine and refused to tell even his wife where it was. It has not been found to this day.

Washoe County—Johnny Calico was a Paiute Indian doctor who lived at Pyramid Lake. His granddaughter told that he had buried a large bag of gold coins beneath a rock on the shore of the lake, but she did not know exactly where. It is generally believed that the treasure was secreted at the point on the lake nearest the town of Nixon.

Washoe County—Sometime in the 1860's, a small Chinese wagon train made camp at the southern tip of Pyramid Lake. The Orientals had come from California where they had successfully worked over mining claims left by other miners. Aware that impatient whites seldom remove all the gold from a mine, the Chinese frequently gleaned considerable wealth from abandoned claims. The Chinese camped at Lake Pyramid had prospered in this manner and had accumulated two chests of gold coins which were being transported in one of their three wagons. They were now headed for the mining camp of Tuscarora where they would work over more claims left by Americans.

Early on the morning of their first day in the camp, a band of Paiute Indians attacked the Chinese miners and killed them all. The Indians removed the food and clothing from the wagons. But scorning the two chests of gold coins, they carried them to the base of a cliff along the lake and buried them.

This story was told in 1923 by an old Indian who said he had participated in the massacre as a boy. Although many searches have been made at the southern tip of Pyramid Lake, no gold has been found. Since the water of the lake has gradually receded, it is believed that the treasure now lies farther from the shore.

Washoe County—On August 2, 1868, the Portland-bound stagecoach out of Boise, Idaho, was robbed by four men at Pelican Station in the Blue Mountains. Wells Fargo was shipping a chest of $7,000 in gold bars. An Army Paymaster was carrying more than $50,000, and the passengers' purses and jewelry brought the haul to a total of more than $64,000. The four highwaymen made their escape but were closely pursued and forced to bury their weighty loot.

When a posse caught up with them, they were arrested and jailed in the Nevada State Prison at Carson City. There one of the prisoners became ill and, knowing that he was going to die, told a guard who had befriended him where to find the loot. He drew a rough map showing that it was buried close to the scene of the robbery.

Quitting his job, the guard hurried to Idaho and found the treasure just as the dying man had said he would. But he was afraid to use money. Since it would attract attention and be seized by the authorities, he took it to a spot near Reno and reburied it. He then located an underworld character in San Francisco and offered to sell the treasure at a big discount. The underworld character demanded to see one of the gold bars before completing the deal. He met the guard on a San Francisco-Oakland ferry. As the guard handed him the gold bar, it slipped from their hands and fell overboard into the bay.

Deciding that he was being bilked, the would-be purchaser reported the matter to the police. The guard was arrested and charged with attempting to defraud with a false brick—as indeed he was. Eleven more of his fake bars were found, and the whole treasure story was discredited. But the Idaho stage robbery was real. The guard had simply used the well-publicized incident as the background for his rascality. Stories are still written about the $64,000 buried near Reno. Did the guard ever retrieve his treasure, or is it still there?

Washoe County—In 1852, a California-bound emigrant wagon train camped at the eastern edge of Granite Range, north of Granite Peak and South of Fox Point. The party was in need of meat and three men were selected to go hunting in the mountains. One of these hunters was a man named John Forman.

The next morning, before starting on their hunt, the three men arranged to meet the wagon train that night at its new camp. Game was scarce and the men kept climbing until they reached the crest of the mountain. From this vantage point, they looked across the valley to the west and saw what they thought was an Indian smoke signal. As they walked down the mountain, being careful to keep out of sight of the Indians, Forman dropped some distance behind his two companions and was somewhat higher up the slope when he stepped on a metallic substance. It was protruding from a large slab of black lava and gray pumice. He called to the other two men and they came back to examine it with him. Forman was inclined to believe it was silver. The others disagreed. With their knives they cut away pieces of the metal, pocketed them, and went on their way in search of game.

Later in the afternoon they again had a view of the valley and realized that what they thought to be Indian signal smoke was in reality vapor from hot springs. The springs are now known as Granite Creek Hot Springs. The men found no game and rejoined the wagons which had made camp at Mud Meadows.

Several days afterward, Forman found that the metal taken from the ledge melted easily and molded some of it into bullets. He was, however, still convinced that it was silver.

The wagon train arrived at its destination in California and Forman forgot all about his unidentified metal until he chanced to see some samples of pure lead. Now he knew that the slab he had seen five or six years before was not silver but pure lead. Having had little success in the gold fields, he made plans to exploit the ledge of lead but kept his intentions to himself.

Before he could leave California, however, he met a Missourian who told him of a supposed lead deposit seen by one of the men in John Fremont's exploration party. The discoverer had told the Missourian its location and drawn a rough map for him. One of the landmarks was hot springs some distance away. Forman thought that the slab of lead described by the Missourian was the same outcropping he had seen. But when the man declared his intention of looking for the metal in the spring, Forman said nothing of his own plans for prospecting.

Early in the spring of 1859, Forman was back at the spot where he and his companions had camped years before at the foot of the mountain. While arranging his camp, he noted that someone had camped there only a day or two before.

Early the next morning he was climbing through the mountains when he looked down across the valley toward the hot springs and saw the Missourian below him on the slope. They met and each man accused the other of bad faith. Arriving at no agreement, they continued their independent searches, and both were unsuccessful.

The following year, and for several years thereafter, both men made further searches for the lost lead deposit. The Missourian declared that Forman had found it and covered it up. Forman made the same charge against the Missourian, and the ledge of lead may still be unexploited.

TREASURE GUIDE

White Pine County—Somewhere in the Ruby Mountains, near the southern tip of Ruby Lake, must lie a lost gold mine originally found by a pioneer named Joshua Ward. Ward, along with his wife and two children, was killed at their cabin by Indians in 1878. Their remains were not found in the isolated spot until some thirty years later when a search for the Wards was instigated by relatives in Massachusetts.

In the yard of the dilapidated cabin was a sagging wagon holding two tons of rich gold ore, untouched and probably unseen since the massacre of the Ward family. After sending the remains of the family east for burial, members of the search party made extensive efforts to locate the source of Ward's gold. According to reports, it was never found.

NEVADA

METAL DETECTOR SITES

Churchill County—East Gate is an almost deserted village to the south of US 50 about midway between Austin and Fallon. For years it was a crude stage station at the mouth of a narrow canyon. Then it was acquired by George Williams and developed into the most noted stopping place in that part of Nevada. It became also a favorite camping ground for Indians who held huge celebrations there.

A short distance west of the village is a narrow pass through low hills which was once called Middlegate. It was the site of a Pony Express Station and later a stage stop. The spot may be difficult to locate.

Churchill County—Inquiry should be made in the almost-deserted town of Frenchman, once called Frenchman's Station, for directions to the ghost town of Wonder. Ore was discovered there in 1906, and for a few years it was the most important producer of gold and silver in the region. The remains of a large mill overlook the ruins of the town where single lots once sold for $8,000. Later, the same lots could not be given away.

Churchill County—Inquiry should be made in Fallon (US 50-95) for directions to the site of Sand Springs near US 50 about 23 miles to the east. This was an early and popular stage line stop. Nothing remains of it today.

Churchill County—Inquiry should be made in Fallon for directions to the crumbling buildings in the village once called Fairview. This early twentieth century camp stood on three successive sites, being moved each time for a more advantageous location. Little evidence remains of the first two sites.

Fairview boomed in the spring of 1906 after silver had been discovered on the slope of Fairview Peak. The town boasted a bank, a hotel, mercantile stores, assay offices, drug stores, bakeries, a newspaper, union hall, dancehall, and 27 saloons. Within two months after the camp's founding, it had a population of 2,000.

The shell of the old stamp mill still stands. Its machinery was dismantled after mining operations ceased in 1918. Soon there were only two persons in Fairview, Ed and Sylvia Stratton, who came there in 1914. If they are still there, they will show visitors to the three sites of Fairview.

Churchill County—On both sides of US 50 about 15 miles west of Fallon above the flat lands lie the slopes of low hills in the distance. These are the terraces of ancient Lake Lahontan, one of the outstanding geological features of the Great Basin. 600 to 2,000 years ago, Indians lived along the shoreline of the lake. Burial grounds, petroglyphs, arrowheads, and other primitive weapons have been found in the area.

Churchill County—What remains of the town of Stillwater is on State Highway 42 a short distance northwest of Fallon. In emigrant days, a toll road was built across an arm of the Carson Sink there, and in 1868 the small community became the seat of Churchill County. When Fallon acquired the county seat in 1902, Stillwater became chiefly a village of Indians, and most of these are gone today.

Churchill County—Inquiry should be made in Fallon for directions to the deserted town of Letteville, first called Ragtown. Ragtown became a station of the Overland Road and remained a stopping place after the Simpson Road came into use. Numerous traders camped there in the summer, and it was there that many travelers discarded possessions to lighten their loads before starting the steep climb into the Sierras. Sometimes, as many as five or six wagon trains camped together on the banks of the Humboldt River near Ragtown. The travelers were all trying to rest and regain strength for the last great effort. All kinds of wagons, farming implements, and household goods were abandoned.

Churchill County—Other ghost towns and possible ghosts: Desert (41); Hazen; Carson Sink Station; Victor; Mirage (35); Wildcat Station; Bernice (50); Terrill; Shady Run; Eagle Salt Works (25); Coppereid; Salt Wells; La Plata; Fillmore; Healy (30); Hill; Hercules; Silver Hill; Dixie Valley; Bolivia; Cold Springs; St. Clair (159); Clan Alpine; Jessup; White Plains (28).

Clark County—The ghost town of Nelson, sometimes known as Eldorado, is on State Highway 60 between Searchlight and Boulder City. Spaniards are said to have discovered valuable minerals in this section of Eldorado Canyon about 1775.

The mine and its satellites produced several millions in gold, silver, copper and lead before disagreements over ownership and management along with labor disputes and a series of wanton killings contributed to the camp's decline. The huge vats used for processing gold ore stand rotting in the blistering heat of the canyon.

Clark County—Inquiry should be made in Searchlight on US 95 for directions to the ghost town of Crescent which is just off State Highway 68 to the west. Turquoise was discovered there in 1894. Small amounts of lead, silver, copper and other metals were also produced. Today, a smoke-blackened fireplace and chimney of a single home are all that mark the site of Crescent.

Clark County—Other ghost towns and possible ghosts: Potosi; Sandy; Platina; Crystal Park; Clarks (37); Alumite; Sunset; West Point; Eldorado Canyon (250); Mountain Springs; St. Joseph; Kaolin; Junction City; Gold Butte.

Douglas County—Inquiry should be made in Carson County for directions to Summit Camp, about eight miles to the southwest. During the 1870's, this was an important stage stop and wood camp.
Another stage station nearby was Spooner's, a short distance to the west.

Douglas County—Inquiry should be made in Stateline (US 50) for directions to the ghost town of Fridays, or Small's Station, about one mile to the east. Originally a Pony Express stop, Fridays gained considerable importance as a station on the Lake Bilger toll road after its completion in 1863. Many years later, the place became known as Edgewood. The ruins of a small building or two are about all that mark the site.

Douglas County—Glenbrook is 11 miles north of Stateline. The first permanent settlement on Lake Tahoe, it became an important lumbering town and supplied the Comstock mines. In 1885 it had a population of 335. It boasted four sawmills, stores, a billiard hall and bowling alley. When the lumbering ceased in the late 1890's, old Glenwood passed away. The small present-day resort and residential community stands in its place.

Douglas County—Other ghost towns and possible ghosts: Van Sickles; Mottsville; Holbrook (50), once known also as Burnt Cabin and Mountain House; Wheelers, also known as Tisdell and Twelvemile House; Sheridan (107); Carter's Station; Double Spring.

Elko County—Inquiry should be made in Battle Mountain (Interstate 80) for directions to the ghost town of Midas on unimproved State 18 to the north. Gold was discovered there in 1907, and the town soon grew to a population of 5,000. It had a newspaper, a chamber of commerce, city water system, four general stores, several hotels, rooming houses, and numerous saloons. The post office closed in 1942, and most of the mines a short time later. Today, the town is deserted and only a few sagging buildings remain standing.

Elko County—The present town of Contact is on US 93 fifty miles north of Wells. The original site of the town, then known as Contact City, was three-quarters of a mile to the west. In 1925, Contact City had a population of 260 with several stores and saloons. When copper prices fell, what remained of the town dropped its illusory "City," changed its name to Contact, and moved to its present site.

Elko County—Inquiry should be made in the almost-deserted town of Montello (State 30) for directions to Emigrant Springs about 32 miles distant. For those on the westward treks, Emigrant Springs was a much-used camping place on the Fort Hall Road. It was where travelers discarded expendable items to lighten the loads of their weakened animals. Many relics have been found in the area.

Elko County—Inquiry should be made in Montello for directions to the almost-abandoned town of Cobre. Laid out primarily as a railroad junction town, Cobre never attained more than 60 population, but had a store, hotel, saloon, railroad station and several houses. Cobre dwindled with its decreasing railroad traffic. The post office closed in 1956. A few cabins and a scattering of people are all that is left of Cobre.

Elko County—The completely deserted town of Toano is two miles northwest of Cobre. This once important railroad division point and eating stop was also a center for freighting and staging supplies into many Idaho and Nevada mining camps. Railroad repair shops and a roundhouse largely supported the town of 250 people. There were several saloons, a boarding house, mercantile store, post office, and other buildings. Many of those buildings were constructed of sandstone blocks. When the railroad discontinued its repair shops there, numerous buildings were moved to the new junction point at Cobre. Then the railroad doubled its tracks through Toano and its deserted stone structures were destroyed. Only the cemetery remains.

Elko County—Inquiry should be made in Oasis (US 40) for directions to Flowery Lake which is about 10 miles south of the near-ghost town of Shafter. In this grass-covered, spring-fed swamp, the Donner party paused long enough in 1846 to cache belongings in order to lighten their wagons. It is believed that these articles have never been recovered.

Fremont camped there in 1845 and called the place Whitton Springs.

Elko County—One of the principal camping spots on the California Trail was northwest of Wells (US 40-93). Travelers called the springs there "wells," giving the town its name. Before the coming of the railroad, hundreds of pioneers stopped their wagon trains at Wells to rest and fatten their animals before starting the long journey down the Humboldt.

Elko County—The town of Deeth (US 40) can still be found on maps although it has virtually disappeared. As a shipping point, supply center, and headquarters for many ranches scattered over a wide area, Deeth prospered and attained a population of 250. There were schools, stores, saloons, a newspaper, a Mormon church, blacksmith shop, livery stable, barbershop and other institutions. In 1915 a fire destroyed the major part of the town and started its decline. Today, there is only one store and a few inhabitants.

Elko County—Inquiry should be made in Wells for directions to the old town of Charleston on Seventy-Six Creek to the north. The discovery of gold at the base of Copper Mountain in 1876 led to the founding of the camp that was first called Mardis. Mardis grew rapidly and soon had several stores, saloons, a hotel and other businesses. For many years the town had the reputation of being the toughest in Nevada. Only two or three caved-in log cabins on a private ranch mark its site.

Elko County—The remains of the old town of White Rock are along State 11 south of Owyhee. At one time, the place had a population of 100 with a few stores and a saloon serving the nearby ranches. Its post office closed in 1925, and all that is left of White Rock is the ruins of a few foundations on a private ranch.

Elko County—Inquiry should be made in Owyhee (State 11-51) for directions to Deep Creek, an old stage station and ghost town on State 11 to the south. In 1872, when gold was discovered in the Cornucopia District to the west, a camp quickly sprang up at Deep Creek. Although the mines produced more than $1,000,000, the town had but a brief life. It is now in complete ruins.

Elko County—Inquiry should be made in Elko (US 40) for directions to the abandoned town of North Fork on State 51 about 50 miles to the north. It is still shown on some maps. Situated on the North Fork of the Humboldt River, the small hamlet had a population of about 75 in 1910, with a few stores and a school. The post office closed in 1944, and the place was gradually abandoned.

Elko County—Inquiry should be made in Owyhee for directions to the site of the ghost town of Bruno City. To the east of the Bruneau River, it began as a mining camp after the discovery of gold and silver on Silver Mountain. In 1870, the camp had a population of 125. Better mining prospects at White Pine and Mountain City attracted its miners, and Bruno City was abandoned.

Elko County—All that remains of the once bustling town of Jarbidge is on an unnamed road north of Wells close to the Idaho border. It was the most isolated of all Nevada mining camps. News of a fabulous gold strike made there in 1909 swelled Jarbidge to a population of about 1,500 within six weeks. But the reports of the discovery had been grossly exaggerated, and after

TREASURE GUIDE

a few months many people had left. Jarbidge boomed once again in 1911 and attained a population of 1,200 before it declined. Nevertheless, it was for a number of years the chief producer of gold in Nevada. Several cabins, a few stone ruins, and about a dozen permanent residents are all that is left of the town.

Elko County—Inquiry should be made in Owyhee for directions to the almost deserted town of Rowland on the east bank of the Bruneau River almost on the Idaho line.

Elko County—Inquiry should be made in Owyhee for directions to the abandoned mining camp of Gold Creek to the southeast. A false rumor of a gold strike there caused a rush of people to the place, and the camp sprang up overnight with predictions that it would become Nevada's largest city in a few years. The buildings included a three-story hotel, post office, stage depot, lodging houses, various stores and a dozen saloons. Several doctors, assayers, engineers and architects opened offices. But by 1900 the district was almost deserted. Gold in paying quantities had failed to materialize. Though some placer mining continued for several years, all of Gold Creek's buildings had been moved away by 1928. A cemetery, a few cellars, and broken slabs of sidewalk are all that identify the site today.

Elko County—Inquiry should be made in Elko (US 40) for directions to a place called Dinner Station. It is about 27 miles north of Elko at the junction of State Highway 11 and 51. The two-story stone structure flanked by ranch buildings was once a favorite stop for meals on the road to the ranches and mines of northern Elko County.

Elko County—Inquiry should be made in Wells (US 40) for directions to Metropolis, about 14 miles to the northwest. When a great reclamation project was planned for this area, it was predicted that Metropolis would grow to a modern city of 7,500 people. The idea caught fire in 1909, and by 1911 the town had graded streets, broad concrete sidewalks, street lights and a four-block commercial district. More than 700 eager settlers flocked in to buy land. The town soon had a post office, a wagon factory, five saloons, and a $75,000 modern brick hotel. But in 1912 the promoters of Metropolis lost a court decision giving them the water from certain creeks necessary to sustain the community, and the project was doomed. Today, Metropolis is hardly more than a name on a map.

Elko County—The ghost town of Tuscarora is on State 11 northwest of Elko where inquiry concerning it should be made. Tuscarora was the chief camp of a mining district on the eastern slope of Mount Blitzen..During the town's heyday, several thousand people lived there, including 2,000 Chinese who had been imported to work on the building of the Central Pacific Railroad. Before this tough camp declined, it had produced $40,000,000 worth of

NEVADA

ore, mostly silver. Only ruins of the old town remain.

Elko County—The nearly-deserted town of Halleck Station (sometimes called only Halleck) is south of US 40 about seven miles east of Elko. The town was built on the Humboldt River to serve Fort Halleck. The post was closed in 1866, and only scattered foundations of the town remain.

The almost-vanished town of Arthur is a few miles south of Halleck.

Elko County—Inquiry should be made in Elko for directions to the ghost town of Cornucopia about 55 miles to the northwest. The discovery of silver there in 1872 resulted in a stampede to the spot and the founding of the camp with a population of almost 1,000 by 1874. The town had drugstores, chop houses, lodging houses, saloons and a 30-room hotel. Two mills processed the mines' ores. The burning of the mills coincided with the decline in the price of silver, and the town succumbed. By 1880 only 170 people remained in Cornucopia, and these soon drifted away. About all that remains are the mill ruins south of the townsite.

Elko County—The ghost town of Edgemont sprang up when gold was discovered on the west slope of the Bull Run Mountains. Mining continued until 1917, when an unusually severe snowslide demolished the mill and the camp's principal buildings. Its post office closed in 1918. Directions to its ruins can be obtained in Elko.

Elko County—Many relics of the westward trek have been found about five miles west of where US 40 crosses the Humboldt River. Several Indian attacks on wagon trains occurred along this stretch of road.

Elko County—Ore was discovered at Bullion in 1869 on the east slopes of the Pinon Mountains. The district produced $3,000,000 in ore before 1884, and by 1885 the town had a population of 400. Production was declining by the end of the century, but activity revived in 1916 and 1917. When the ores decreased again, so did Bullion. Directions to its ruins can be obtained in Elko.

Elko County—Inquiry should be made in Elko for directions to the small town of Lamoille. From Lamoille, a Forest Service road leads into the Humboldt National Forest and farther on into a rugged section of the Ruby Mountains. This road crosses numerous pegmatite dikes in the granite. In those dikes are found garnets, beryl crystals, mica and many other minerals. Among them are some very fine gemstones.

Elko County—The small town of Jiggs is on State 46 south of Elko. It has been called Mound Valley, then Skelton, Hilton and finally Jiggs. In the piñon hills to the west of Jiggs, Indians once maintained year-round camps, and many relics have been found in the area.

Elko County—Inquiry should be made in Jiggs (State 46) for directions to the site of Camp Ruby. Also known as Fort Ruby, it is now on a private ranch. A trading post was operated at Camp Ruby as early as 1859 by "Uncle" Billy Rogers. In 1862, the fort was established as the military headquarters along that section of the Overland Stage Route. Camp Ruby was a stage station, a change post for the Pony Express, and eventually a relay base for telegraph messages.

Elko County—Other ghost towns and near ghosts: Lee (150); Falcon; Ivada; Clover Valley (42); Mountain City; Patsville; Huntington (47); Loray (37); Rio Tinto; Aura; Moleen (38); Poquop (31); Sprucemound (34); Shephard's Station; Ruby City; Tecoma (60); Tulasco (60); Cedar (22); Buel; Bishops (37); Blaine (30); Currie (75); Columbia (75); Fariplay; Dolly Varden; Kingsley; Good Hope; Independence (37); Island Mountain (30); Otego (27); Jasper.

Esmeralda County—The mining town of Silverpeak still has a few inhabitants, but at one time it boasted a population of 4,000. Gold and silver ore was discovered on nearby Red Mountain in 1863, but the boom did not develop until 1906 when the mines began efficient operation. The town sits on the edge of a sink in Clayton Valley on the eastern side of Silver Peak Range. After the original discovery, a 10-stamp mill was built. But the community almost expired and did not revive until eastern interests assumed control of the mines. The ore began to decrease in 1915. A year later, the owners moved mill and railroad to California and reduced the town to its present status.

Esmeralda County—A town of 300 is hardly a ghost, but when that town once boasted 10,000 people, there are certainly ghosts in its shadows.

Gold was discovered at Goldfield in 1902, and in less than a year it was a town of 10,000 population. It had a stock exchange and city lots sold for $45,000. In 1910, a 270-room hotel was built. Before the boom faded, Goldfield's mines had produced $150,000,000 in gold.

Goldfield is on US 95. It is probably the best preserved and best protected near-ghost town in the west. An array of substantial buildings still stand in good condition. Many of these have boarded-up windows and padlocked doors. Relic hunters in these buildings are not welcome, but there are places in the town where the hobby can be pursued with the permission of property owners.

On September 13, 1913, Goldfield suffered a devastating flash flood. Water rolled off the rimrock to the west and came roaring through the main part of town. Scores of houses and business buildings crumpled, and the water carried before it all manner of personal property. Included in the still-buried possessions are a few heavy safes, jewelry, cookie jars full of coins, and articles every well-appointed 1913 home and store might have contained. In 1923, ten years after the flood, a disastrous fire burned out 52 city blocks in the lower part of town. Today this district is a brush-covered jungle of crumbling foundations.

Esmeralda County—Inquiry should be made in Goldfield for directions to the ghost town of Blair. A silver strike was made there and a townsite laid out. By 1910, Blair's population was about 2,000. On a hill above the town, a 25-stamp mill was built. The town had schools, newspapers, saloons, hotels, a church and a bank. In 1915, after nine years of production in which the mines had yielded $7,000,000, the ores were exhausted and mining ceased. The ruins of Blair are amid an indescribable amount of debris. Only the skeletons of three concrete buildings remain where once stood a hundred or more. The locations of several saloons are indicated by huge mounds of broken bottles.

Esmeralda County—The remains of the mining camp of Gold Reef lie about six miles southeast of Tonopah (US 6-95). A gold strike was made there in 1909, and a few buildings were erected. The camp lasted less than a year and practically nothing marks the site today.

Esmeralda County—Inquiry should be made in Goldfield for directions to the ghost town of Diamondfield. The town was laid out in 1903 by "Diamondfield" Davis, soon after he had received an eleventh-hour pardon for a murder conviction. At its height in 1904, the town had a post office, a restaurant, school, church, butcher shop, miners' union hall, assay office, blacksmith shop, two general stores and three saloons. Though Diamondfield rivaled Goldfield in production of ore, it never attained more than 300 population. All that stands today are two large stone dwellings amid crumbling rock walls and foundations.

Esmeralda County—Tule Canyon is about 15 miles long. It lies to the west of US 95 in the extreme southeastern corner of Esmeralda County. Mexicans mined there as early as 1848, before the arrival of Americans. Indians and Chinese also worked the extensive placers. Although only about $1,000,000 were taken out of the canyon, it spawned three mining camps, Tule Canyon, Senner and Roosevelt Well. Stone ruins, mine shafts and placer dumps are scattered throughout the canyon.

Esmeralda County—Inquiry should be made in Goldfield for directions to the ruins of Weepah. Indians discovered gold there in 1902, and about 200 people rushed to the site. But little came of it. The place was abandoned until 1927 when two young men rediscovered the gold. It was a fabulous strike, assaying $70,000 to the ton. When the find was known, a stampede began. In a few months Weepah had 60 frame buildings housing the usual line of mining-town businesses. When the excitement subsided the get-rich-quick prospectors left Weepah in disgust. Large mining operations took control, the region was soon worked out, and Weepah collapsed. Only wooden ruins mark the site.

Esmeralda County—Inquiry should be made in Tonopah (US 6-95) for directions to the ghost town of Crow Springs. Beginning in 1902, Crow Springs was an overnight stopping place for teamsters and the main stagecoach stop between Sodaville and Tonopah. Some turquoise was mined there after 1909. but little remains today to indicate the site.

Esmeralda County—Directions to the near-ghost town of Lida can be obtained in Goldfield. Lida is on State 3 about midway between the California boundary and Nye County line. The town has also been known as Lida City, Lida Valley and Alida. Indians and Mexicans mined there as early as 1860, but it had its real beginning in 1872 when Americans discovered ore. It was known as a tough camp with the nearest law enforcement agency 100 miles away. At its peak, the population of the town reached 6,000. Its business center included a bank, a newspaper, several lodging houses, seven stores, twelve saloons, nine restaurants, five feed yards, two assay offices and two blacksmith shops. By 1906, diminishing ores brought the decline of prosperity. The bank failed and miners began moving away. Then came the panic of 1907, and Lida died. What remains of it is now on a private ranch.

Esmeralda County—The ghost town of Klondyke is about 11 miles south of Tonopah, where information concerning it can be obtained. Gold and silver were discovered in Klondike in 1899, but the minin gcamp never amounted to much. Its population was hardly more than 100. Only ruins of wooden buildings mark the site.

Esmeralda County—Inquiry should be made in Oasis, California (State 266) for directions to the ghost town of Palmetto. It is barely across the Nevada line.

Silver was discovered in 1866 at the head of Palmetto Wash. Within a year, Palmetto had a 12-stamp mill, and later a small military garrison was established to protect its citizens from the Indians. About all that remains of the town that produced $6,500,000 in bullion are the roofless stone walls of the post office and stagecoach station, both buildings now overgrown with brush.

A new town called New Palmetto sprang up two miles down the canyon in 1907, but it was unsuccessful. Only a few stone foundations and piles of tin cans mark its site.

The remains of the ghost town of Sylvania are about five miles from old Palmetto almost on the California-Nevada line.

Esmeralda County—Inquiry should be made in Lida (State 3) for directions to the ghost town of Pigeon Springs, about 29 miles to the west. The

NEVADA

small settlement that grew up around the Pigeon stamp mill was short-lived and never amounted to more than a few business buildings and dwellings. Only the mill foundations remain.

Esmeralda County—Inquiry should be made in Pahrump (State 52) for directions to the ghost town of Gold Point. When it was founded in 1866, Gold Point was known as Lime Point. Later it became Horn Silver. It had a peak population of 2,000, but the town was deserted when the great strike was made at Goldfield. In 1908, a high-grade horn silver was discovered in the area, and Gold Point revived. But all mining effort ceased there in 1942. Today about 50 deserted and windowless wooden buildings face the empty streets.

Esmeralda County—Directions to the ghost town of Montezuma can be obtained in Tonopah. Although Indians and Mexicans mined silver there in the 1850's, Americans did not become active in the vicinity until 1867. They built a mill, but all operations ceased in 1907. Remnants of a few buildings are all that are left at the site.

Esmeralda County—Inquiry should be made in Goldfield for directions to the ghost town of Alkali Spring. It was a favorite spa for the social life of Goldfield. The spa was the scene of their picnics, dances and parties. The resort closed in 1918, and only foundations remain.

The camp of Phillipsburg, now a complete ghost, was approximately five miles west of Alkali Spring. It consisted of a few wooden buildings and many tent dwellings. Nothing remains of the camp.

Esmeralda County—Since the ghost town of Columbia is only one mile to the north of Goldfield, it is actually a suburb. It was named for the neighboring Columbia Mountains. By 1907, Columbia had a population of 1,500. But when the large mines in the district closed in 1918, Columbia expired. Acres of foundations, cellars and brick walls attest to its former affluence.

Esmeralda County—Inquiry should be made in Goldfield for directions to the ghost town of Gold Mountain. Gold Mountain is sometimes known as State-Line for the mine of that name. The original strike was made there in 1866, but not until its development in 1872 did it become a lively camp. By 1881 the town had a chop house, livery stable, bakery, butcher shop, two stores, five saloons, and several wooden, canvas and dugout dwellings. Mining declined in 1891, and after a brief revival in 1905 the camp succumbed. All that is left of Gold Mountain are stone ruins, tumbled wooden buildings and the fronts of hillside dugouts.

Esmeralda County—The old town of Coaldale is about one mile from the present-day Coaldale (US 6-95). Coaldale came into being with the discovery of coal in the mountains to the south and was a stagecoach stop for the coal mines. All that remained of the original Coaldale by 1959 was a single service station and many depressions where buildings once stood.

Esmeralda County—The desert mining camp of Oriental was also known at one time as Old Camp and later as Gold Mountain for the slopes on which it was built. Information concerning Oriental can be obtained in Goldfield.

The strike at Oriental is said to have been made by a party searching for the Lost Breyfogle Mine, and for awhile many people believed it was the Breyfogle find of 1864. The camp never grew very large because of its remoteness and lack of water for milling. Only a few roofless buildings and rock ruins are left.

Esmeralda County—Inquiry should be made in Coaldale for directions to the ghost town of Fish Lake, once known also as Borax City. This place should not be confused with the Fish Lake shown on modern highway maps. After borax operations started at Fish Lake in 1875, the village grew to about 200 people and about 40 buildings. By 1880 the town was dead. Only a few foundations remain.

Esmeralda County—The ghost town of Cuprite was founded in 1903 when copper was discovered in the hills to the north. Directions to it may be obtained at .Goldfield. A railroad reached Cuprite in 1906, and the town became a shipping center for several neighboring mining camps. By 1910 mining activities had declined, and Cuprite was all but deserted. Only a few foundations mark the site.

Esmeralda County—Other ghost towns and possible ghosts: Coryville (40); Elbow Station; Fletcher (25); Garfield (25); Nine Mile House (25); Six Mile House; Soda Springs; Divide; Gold Reef; Royston; Nivoloc; Gold Hitt.

Eureka County—The town of Eureka is on US 50. It is the seat of Eureka County and far from a ghost, but at its peak of mining production it boasted 10,000 population. It was an important railroad center. In a 14-year period its mines produced $40,000,000 in silver, $20,000,000 in gold, and 225,000 pounds of lead. In 1919, more than 30 miles of railroads were washed out by a flood, depriving the town of its lucrative trade. Bank failures added to the misfortune, and a drop in lead and silver prices led to the abandonment of so many large holdings that miners left for more prosperous centers. Foundations and stone structures dating back as far as 1869 are visible for miles around the present town. Idle smelters and deserted houses stand as reminders of Eureka's former opulence.

Two miles to the west of Eureka is the ghost town of Ruby Hill, which once had a population of 2,165. The town had many fine buildings, all of which were abandoned when mining operations in the area ceased.

Eureka County—Inquiry should be made in Eureka for directions to the ghost town of Buckhorn, about 40 miles to the northwest. After gold was discovered on the slopes of the Cortez Mountains near there, a camp was established and rapidly grew to a population of 300. The town supported saloons, several stores, a hotel, livery stable and other business establishments. When the vein pinched out in 1916, Buckhorn was abandoned. Very little evidence of the town can be located today.

Eureka County—The ghost town of Mineral Hill is about 30 miles south of Carlin (US 40), where directions to its ruins can be obtained.

In 1869, when silver float was discovered in Mineral Hill, a camp rapidly developed around it. A year later, the district had about 500 people with their stores, restaurants, saloons, meat market, bakery and other businesses. By 1872, the main deposits were worked out and miners started drifting away. Only mill foundations and a few crumbling buildings survive.

Eureka County—About 11 miles south of Carlin, the town of Palisade stood in a picturesque canyon. It had about 600 population when it was the northern terminus of the Eureka & Palisade Railroad which brought gold and silver bullion from the mining camps of the county. An array of stores, saloons, hotels and other commercial establishments served its residents and travelers. In 1910, heavy floods destroyed much of the town, and with the abandonment of the railroad, Palisade had no hope of recovery. Only a few wrecked wooden buildings and stone ruins remain.

This region was long a favorite Paiute Indian campsite. The tribe maintained an all-year camp near the hot springs and geysers to the south. Many relics have been gathered in the vicinity.

Eureka County—Inquiry should be made in Carlin for directions to Safford, 14 miles to the southwest. Silver was discovered there in 1883, and a small camp developed, but its life was short. Hardly anything remains to mark its site.

Eureka County—The ghost town of Union is about 32 miles south of Carlin, where information concerning it can be obtained.

Lead-silver ore was discovered in Union in 1880, and a small company town developed near the mine. It was never more than a few buildings. When operations declined in 1918, the town was abandoned. Scattered ruins are the only evidence of its existence.

Eureka County—Inquiry should be made in Carlin for directions to Blackburn, about 37 miles to the south. Situated on the Eureka & Palisade Railroad, the town thrived for a few years. But it died with the decline of mining in the area. Since all buildings were moved to other camps, nothing but foundations remain in Blackburn.

Eureka County—The ghost town of Alpha is about 40 miles north of Eureka, where directions to it can be obtained.

As the southern terminus of the Eureka & Palisade Railroad, Alpha had large railroad shops, freight barns, a commodious depot, numerous stores and a hotel. But when the railroad moved to the south in 1875, the town's usefulness was ended. By 1880, most of the residents were gone. Cellar depressions alone mark the site.

Eureka County—Other ghost towns and possible ghosts: Philipsburg; Columbia; Pine Station (123); Gerald (45); Prospect; Vanderbilt; Pinto Mills (40); Diamond City.

Humboldt County—Cane Springs is in the Santa Rosa Range about 23 miles north of Winnemucca, where information concerning it can be obtained. For many years, Cane Springs was a popular stop for stagecoaches and travelers. Accommodations included a hotel, saloon and livery stable. The site may be difficult to locate.

Humboldt County—Inquiry should be made in Winnemucca (US 50) for directions to the ghost town of Jumbo and two nearby abandoned camps known as Awakening and Daveytown. About 1910, mining activity began in that vicinity, and three mills were built. Today, only the foundations of the mills and a few scattered ruins indicate where Jumbo, Awakening and Daveytown once thrived.

Humboldt County—The near-ghost town of Golconda is on US 40 about 16 miles east of Winnemucca. The hot springs there were a noted landmark for travelers during the days of the westward trek. When copper mines were developed in the district, Golconda boomed. But the copper ore was soon exhausted. By 1900, all the mines were closed. Golconda now has a population of about 200. Several old, ramshackle buildings and some of the mill foundations still stand.

Humboldt County—Inquiry should be made in Golconda for directions to the ruins of the Stone House Station. Stone House Station was an early mail station. On Treaty Hill just north of the ruins of the stone house, numerous battles were fought between different Indian tribes over the springs and hunting grounds of Battle Mountain and Humboldt Valley. Many relics have been gathered on those grounds.

Humboldt County—Inquiry should be made in Winnemucca for directions to what is left of the old mining camp of Gold Run, also known as

Adelaide and Cumberland. The town laid out there in 1867 never exceeded more than 100 population. It disappeared entirely after mining operations ceased in the region.

Humboldt County—The remains of Camp McGarry on the shores of Summit Lake are in the Summit Lake Indian Reservation in the northwestern corner of Humboldt County. The post was established in 1867 to protect travelers using the Applegate Cutoff to Oregon. Camp McGarry's stone buildings, large storage barn, mess hall and barracks were abandoned in 1871.

Humboldt County—Inquiry should be made at the Summit Lake Indian Reservation for directions to the Virgin Valley Opal Fields. They are difficult to reach. The opals discovered there are generally of the fire variety and are of unexcelled color and brilliance. In 1917, a 17-ounce black opal valued at $25,000 was found. It is now on display in the Smithsonian Institution in Washington, D. C.

Humboldt County—Inquiry should also be made at Summit Lake Indian reservation for directions to the ghost town of Varyville, once known as Columbia. The camp was settled when ores were discovered there in 1875. Five stamp mills were built, but the ore was pinched out by the 1880's and the camp was abandoned. Remnants of some buildings are still standing.

Humboldt County—Information concerning the ghost town of National can be obtained in McDermitt (US 95). Two prospectors discovered gold there in 1907. By 1909, news of the sensational find, which was one of the richest in Nevada, had attracted 2,000 people. By 1911, National had several stores, professional offices, a hotel, post office, newspaper and other establishments. After producing $7,000,000, the camp expired, its rich ore exhausted. Only a few wooden buildings and the shell of a mill still stand.

Humboldt County—Other ghost towns and possible ghosts: Dun Glenn (47); Haas (25); Vicksburg; Sod House; Pueblo; Raspberry Creek (26); Spring City (128); Buckskin; Sulphur; Toll House (25); Willow Point (25); Rebel Creek (150); Willow Creek (75); Dutch Flat; Paradise Valley; Queen City; Laurel; Red Butte.

Lander County—Inquiry should be made in Austin (US 50) for directions to the ghost town of Geneva, about 17 miles to the south. A silver strike there in 1864 drew several hundred people who built stone, log and tent houses. A 20-stamp mill began operations in 1866, but it closed when the ore proved to be of low value. By 1867, Geneva was deserted. Only parts of several stone structures remain.

TREASURE GUIDE

Lander County—Spencer Hot Springs is southeast of Austin, where directions to it can be obtained. In the early boom days, the hot springs were the leading resort in central Nevada. Though accommodations are no longer there, the spot remains a favorite picnic site and campground.

Lander County—Inquiry should be made in Austin for directions to Simpson Park. After serving as a Pony Express Station during 1860-1861, Simpson Park became a stagecoach station with three log houses and a blacksmith shop. All that remains of the stone foundations are on private property.

Lander County—About 7 miles to the southeast of Battle Mountain (Interstate 80) is the ghost town of Copper Basin. Copper Basin was a booming mining camp, and the hills surrounding it are dotted with abandoned copper mines. Now only battered and abandoned buildings stand on its single street.

In the summer of 1857, while a small wagon train was camped at the spring near Copper Basin, its pioneers were massacred by Indians. Soldiers engaged the Indians in a pitched battle, and many relics of the fight have been found in the vicinity.

Lander County—Inquiry should be made in Battle Mountain for directions to Old Battle Mountain and Copper Canyon. Several other mining camps were also in the area. The names of only two of these are known, Betty O'Neal and Lewis, or Lewis Junction. Betty O'Neal had a 100-ton flotation mill and prosperity enough to support a paid baseball team.

Lander County—The ghost town of Galena is on an unimproved road southwest of Battle Mountain, where directions to its ruins can be obtained. Laid out in 1869, the gold camp of Galena boomed to a population of several thousand. Extensive tailing dumps are all that remain of the mill that processed $5,000,000 worth of ore. Only an old cemetery and a few sagging wooden structures indicate the site of the town.

Lander County—Austin is the seat of Lander County on heavily-traveled US Highway 50. It was the mother town of eastern and central Nevada mining. The first rich strike was made there in 1862. In 1863, there were only 366 houses for 10,000 people, and city lots brought $8,000 in gold. Four years later, the town had 11 mills, 3 churches, private schools, and numerous business establishments. By 1880, $50,000,000 worth of gold, silver and lead had been taken from its mines. But the supply was almost depleted. Austin declined with its diminishing riches. After its railroad was abandoned in 1938, the population fell to 500. Collapsing walls of old brick buildings and the ruins of adobe houses dot the present town.

Lander County—Jacobsville, also known as Jacob's Well, is about 8 miles southwest of Austin. Once a Pony Express station, then a maintenance point on the transcontinental telegraph line, Jacobsville became a temporary county seat when Lander County was formed. But the people of the town gradually moved away when Austin became the permanent county seat.

Lander County—Other ghost towns and possible ghosts: Cortez; Bannock; Curtis (30); McCoy; Argenta; Frisbee (150); Hilltop or Kimberly; Pittsburg; Lander; Helena (30); Tenabo; Gold Acres; Clifton; Yankee Blade; Kingston (26); Amador; Ravenswood; Ledlie; Skookum; Canyon City; Bailey (25); Gold Park; Carroll; Dry Creek Station; Guadaljara; Clinton; Mount Airy.

Lincoln County—Inquiry should be made in Caliente (US 93) for directions to the ghost town of Delamar (sometimes spelled De Lamar). Delamar was known as a "widow maker" because three months in its mines were sufficient to produce fatal silicosis caused by the high content of silica in its ores. More than 600 Mormons died there along with many Chinese, Greeks, Italians and others—all victims of the fatal "Delamar Dust."

Delamar was at one time southern Nevada's largest city. Gold was discovered there in 1892, and its mine produced more than $25,000,000. The town had several stores, hospitals, schools, churches, a bank and an opera house.

Fire once wiped out the entire business district, but it was rebuilt. When Tonopah and Goldfield boomed, Delamar, like many of its miners, died. The ruins are jammed halfway up a shallow, rocky canyon above enormous piles of mine tailings. Most of its houses and stores are now merely stone shells along its single narrow street.

Lincoln County—On a private ranch near Delamar are what remains of the town of Crystal Springs. It was the first seat of Lincoln County and once an important stage station. Only a line of cottonwood trees mark its site.

Lincoln County—The ghost town of Hiko is on State Highway 38 four miles north of US 93 and about 43 miles west of Caliente. Hiko was the second seat of Lincoln County. It was founded in 1866 and widely heralded as a mining camp with great possibilities. But little ore was found at the base of Hiko Range, and the county seat was moved to the new boom town of Pioche.

On a hill overlooking the old townsite, a great smokestack looms above the ruins of a mill staring down on deserted buildings, weatherbeaten and rapidly tumbling into decay.

Lincoln County—Other ghost towns and possible ghosts: Highland; Brown (25); Jackrabbit; Rioville (25); Bristol Well; Bristol; Bullionville

(168); Silverhorn; Atlanta; Royal City (100); Clover Valley; Logan; Freyberg; Groom; Ten Point; Fay; Eagle Valley; Spring Valley .

Lyon County—With a population today of about 150, Dayton (US 50) is not quite a ghost, but only the highway keeps it alive. A mill was built there on the banks of the Carson River to treat the ores of the Comstock Lode. It was there too that the Emigrant Trail crossed the Carson Trail. The place was then known as Ponderer's Rest because California-bound wagon trains often halted there while they decided whether to continue westward or turn south. The settlement was first called McMarlin's Station, then Chinatown, Nevada City, Mineral Rapids and finally Dayton. Several of Dayton's original buildings are still standing, deserted and decaying.

Lyon County—Inquiry should be made in Dayton for directions to the site of old Como, a mining camp that reached its peak of popularity in 1864 when it was the seat of Lyon County. Nothing is left of Como.

Lyon County—The ruins of old Fort Churchill loom against the sky on a dirt road running west of Weeks (Alternate US 95). This army post was once the military headquarters of Nevada, an important stagecoach station and a telegraph relay station.

The fort was established on the banks of the Carson River in 1860 to protect wagon trains traveling the old Simpson Trail. By the fall of 1860, Fort Churchill comprised 58 adobe buildings with stone foundations. During the Civil War, it was enlarged and became a recruiting station for Union forces and a prison for Confederate sympathizers. The last troops left in 1869. In 1871, the fort was sold at public auction for $750. The main fort structure, with a few small stables and warehouses, still stands among the ruins of the camp hospital, subsistence store, quartermaster's store, commandant's office and telegraph station. The site of Fort Churchill became the first state park acquired by the State of Nevada.

Lyon County—The ghost town of Ludwig is about 10 miles west of Yerington (Alternate US 95), where directions to its site can be obtained.

Ludwig was a former copper mining camp and one of the best preserved abandoned towns in Nevada until some years ago when the usable remnants were dismantled and sold for scrap. The scrap merchants left nothing but useless rubble.

Lyon County—Inquiry should be made in Wellington (State 3) for directions to the ghost town of Pine Grove, to the southwest. Gold was discovered there in 1866, and within a year the camp had a population of 300. Three mills shipped $10,000 worth of bullion every week, and the population continued to grow until about 1880. By the early 1930's, Pine Grove's ore was depleted and the camp was abandoned.

NEVADA

Lyon County—The almost abandoned town of Silver Peak is 3 miles northwest of Dayton.

Silver Peak was a mining camp established in 1859. It soon became an important place with saloons, boarding houses, four hotels, and large facilities for horses and wagons hauling ore between the Comstock mines and the mills on the Carson River. By 1861, the town had a population of 1,200. When the railroad replaced the horse-and-wagon freighting business, Silver Peak's population gradually declined.

Lyon County—Stone ruins and a historical marker indicate the site of the small placer mining camp of Johntown on State 17. Overshadowed by Virginia City, the camp never attained more than 180 population.

Lyon County—Other ghost towns and possible ghosts: Wabuska (75); Rockland; Cambridge; Hudson; Mound House (50); Summit Station; Reed's Station; Colony; Ramsey; Stockton Well; Cline's Hot Springs; Mason Valley (150); Artesia; Walker River Station; Wiley's Station; Sweetwater; Elbow; Talapoosa; Honey Lake Smith's; Bucklands; Desert Well Station; Thompson.

Mineral County—Inquiry should be made in Mina (US 95) for directions to Belleville. The town came into being in 1873 with the building of the Northern Belle Mill which was soon followed by a second mill. At one time, Belleville's population of 600 supported hotels, saloons, restaurants, two newspapers and other business establishments. When water was piped to the nearby and larger camp of Candelaria, Belleville's mills closed, and the town was doomed. Only foundations and broken walls remain.

Near these ruins the ghost town of Marietta has even fewer remnants of the past.

Mineral County—The remains of Sodaville lie along US 95 a few miles south of Mina. At one time, Sodaville was the most important town between Reno and Tonopah. Its history dates back to the 1880's, when its pig mill processed ores from the famous silver camp of Candelaria. The railroad ended at Sodaville, and all freight for Tonopah had to be transferred to wagons. Fragments of these wagons are still scattered along the road.

Mineral County—A short distance south of the ruins of Sodaville in the Rhodes Salt Marsh, a few tumbled-down buildings mark the site of Rhodes. Rhodes once supplied much of the salt used in roasting non-free-milling silver ore.

Mineral County—Inquiry should be made in Mina for directions to the ghost town of Metallic, also known as Metallic City and called Pickhandle Gulch by the miners who worked in the long, deep canyon. Most of Metallic's houses were built of native stone and empty whiskey cases. The ruins of these and a mill are all that is visible today.

TREASURE GUIDE

Mineral County—On US Highway 95 about 25 miles south of Mina, 7 miles of graded road lead west to Candelaria. It is said to be the dustiest 7 miles in the world. Mexicans discovered silver ore in Candelaria in 1864, but the claim was not developed until 15 years later. Germans, Slavs and Americans replaced the Mexicans, and the building of a railroad attracted many Chinese. By 1800, Candelaria had ten saloons, two hotels, a dozen stores, offices and other buildings.

Before the fall in the price of silver in 1893, Candelaria had produced $33,000,000 and attained a population of 5,000. It was one of Nevada's most famed and prosperous mining camps.

Today, the twisting main street is edged by the strong stone walls of the leading bank, a restaurant, hardware store and the assay building. The two newspaper offices were less sturdy and have crumbled into ruins. A few rusty little cars stand on dismembered rail lengths alongside the old 18-inch gauge mine train, possessively guarding the Carson & Colorado Railroad's abandoned right-of-way. To the right of the cemetery at the east edge of town, a steep two-mile drive leads to Candelaria's suburb of Pickhandle Gulch, where a few old stone buildings still stand.

The elements, vandals, and wreckers seeking materials for building reduced Candelaria to its present state of ruin.

Mineral County—Inquiry should be made in Hawthorne (US 95) for directions to the ghost town of Aurora, to the southwest near the California border. Once called Esmeralda, Aurora was the companion town to notoriously tough Bodie across the border in California. Booming with a population of 10,000 in 1864, Aurora produced $30,000,000 in bullion in less than 10 years. Its business district consisted of 100 or more substantial buildings, many of them brick and stone. A change of state boundary lines gave Aurora the unique distinction of being the seat of Mono County in California and then of Esmeralda County in Nevada.

Known throughout the mining world as a wicked, wild, rich and gory camp, Aurora left nothing to refute its reputation.

Mineral County—Directions to the ghost town of Rawhide can be obtained in Schurz on US 95. Incited by the Goldfield boom, this spectacular camp began in 1906 and mushroomed to a city of 10,000 people in seven months. The financial panic of 1907 and a disastrous fire in 1908 that wiped out nine square blocks in the heart of town hastened Rawhide's decline. A few people still live there with their slowly disintegrating theatre, hotel, post office, stone jail and saloon.

Mineral County—The deserted town of Columbus is on the north edge of the Columbus Salt Marsh near the town of Basalt (US 6). Columbus was the milling town for the Candelaria mines to the north. When the mill closed, Columbus crumbled into ruins.

NEVADA

Mineral County—The small town of Luning is at the junction of US 95 and State 23. In 1879, lead, silver and copper properties were developed a few miles east and northeast of town. The silver mines were worked out in 1893, and copper mining all but ceased after World War I. Today, Luning is reduced to a store and a filling station.

Mineral County—Other ghost towns and possible ghosts: Walker River (50); Simon; Omco; Thorne; Douglass; Garfield; Pamlico; Broken Hills; Bovard; Dead Horse Well; Eagleville; Dutch Creek; Granite; Mountain View; Ore City; Whisky Spring; Lucky Boy.

Nye County—Warm Springs is a hamlet on US 6 about 49 miles east of Tonopah on the eastern slope of the Hot Creek Range. A rock house built there in 1866 was used as a shelter for travelers. For many years it was a stopping place for stagecoaches and freight wagons on the Tonopah-Ely route.

Nye County—Rhyolite was one of the biggest booms in mining history. It came quickly and collapsed fast. Directions to the ghost town can be obtained in Beatty (US 95).

Gold was discovered in Rhyolite in 1905. By 1907, it had a population of about 12,000 and boasted of its many modern stores, newspapers, banks, opera house and countless saloons. The pride of the town was its Union Station which served two of its three railroads. By 1910, the gold vein was depleted and Rhyolite reverted to the sagebrush. Many of its much-lauded buildings were moved away. Others collapsed.

At the foot of Rhyolite's main street are the faint traces of another town, Bullfrog, the first mining camp settled there after gold was discovered.

Nye County—What remains of the mining town of Manhattan, once called Manhattan Gulch, sits in an inviting canyon almost on the slope of Bald Mountain. It can be reached on State 69 north of Tonopah. The camp sprang up in 1906 after gold was discovered, but there had been some activity as early as 1890. A mill was built in 1912 and the town grew to a population of 500 before its decline began. A few people still live there, but most of the town is in ruins.

Nye County—Belmont, one of Nevada's better preserved ghost towns, is on State 82 north of Tonopah where inquiries concerning it can be made.

Belmont developed in 1863 after lead-silver ore was discovered in the district. Two years later, it was the seat of Nye County. In 1885, after it had produced $15,000,000 in gold and silver and 11,000 flasks of mercury, its ores began to decline. Turquoise was discovered there in 1901, and a 10-stamp, 100-ton flotation mill was erected. It lasted only two years. Another stamp mill was built in 1921, but it closed within the year.

The demonetizing of silver struck the first blow against Belmont; then came the great boom at Tonopah, which almost drained the town of people. The final blow came with Tonopah's gaining the county seat. Belmont had built the Nye County courthouse at a cost of $20,000, and it still stands. But after more than a half century, it is succumbing to the forces of nature along with the music hall, large store, jewelry store, assay offices, several cafes, saloons and the tiny stone cabins of Belmont's Chinatown. Today, a few prospectors and Indians occasionally camp there.

Nye County—With a population of about 1,600 today, Tonopah (US 6-95) is hardly a ghost town, but the ghosts of its former mines haunt the scenes of its past. The producer of more than $125,000,000 in gold, Tonopah experienced a boom seldom equalled in western mining history. But by 1930, the population had decreased to little more than 2,000. The town still sits in a bed of rich minerals. The area around it is a veritable gem field, full of petrified wood, jasper and other semi-precious material.

Nye County—Inquiry should be made in Tonopah for directions to the ghost town of Klondyke, about 14 miles to the southeast. Silver, gold, lead and copper ores were discovered there in 1899. No great rush developed, but a small camp grew up which supported a modest business and a post office for several years. The remains of the Klondyke Mine are in a steep, narrow canyon near the crest of the Klondyke Hills. A few buildings are still intact, including the hoist house, gallows frame and the superintendent's home. There are sizeable trash dumps in the canyon below the mine, and flood waters have carried bottles and assorted items a mile or so away from the camp itself.

Nye County—The silver mining town of San Antonio was 35 miles north of Tonopah where inquiries concerning it can be made.

Silver ore was discovered in San Antonio by Mexicans in 1863. In 1865, Americans developed the finds and built a 10-stamp mill. It was dismantled a year later and hauled across the valley to booming Belmont. The post office, established in 1873, was closed in 1888, reopened in 1893, and closed again in 1906, by which time most of San Antonio's population had drifted to newer and larger camps. Today the town is completely deserted.

Nye County—The ghost town of Gilbert is in the Monte Cristo Mountains about 28 miles northwest of Tonopah.

When the Gilbert Brothers discovered gold in 1924, Nevada's last real mining rush began, and Gilbert was the last substantial boom town in the state. Reaching a peak population of 800, the town declined as the ore diminished. By 1929, Gilbert had only 60 people. Today it is completely deserted, its few scattered buildings in ruins.

NEVADA

Nye County—The ruins of the milling town of Millers stand on US 95 about 13 miles west of Tonopah. A rest stop on US 95, Millers has been a favorite spot for bottle and rock collectors for a number of years. Originally known as Desert Wells Station, it was an important watering stop for two freight and stagecoach lines. The coming of the railroad brought an end to freighting, and the stop was no longer needed. After its name was changed to Millers, two large stamp mills were built a half mile south of the town. Its population soon jumped to 300, and a small business section developed. Millers' dream of becoming the largest shipper of bullion in the United States was shattered in 1910 when the first of four mills was built in Tonopah. A few old cabins south of the mill are all that remains of the camp.

Nye County—Inquiry should be made in Tonopah for directions to the old mining camp of Hannapah, about 20 miles to the east. A townsite was laid out there in 1906, but the anticipated town did not materialize. Large holes in the refuse dump attest to the visit of bottle collectors to the ruins.

Nye County—The ghost town of Divide is about 5 miles southeast of Tonopah.
In 1901, when gold was discovered at Divide, a small but active community called Gold Mountain developed. The place should not be confused with the ghost town of Gold Mountain in Esmeralda County. The news of the sensational strikes in Goldfield and Rhyolite lured most of the prospectors to them, and Divide gradually declined. The town, with the post office name of Sigold, had several businesses and saloons. Little remains of Divide except headframes, huge dumps and the foundations of a few buildings.

Nye County—Other ghost towns and possible ghosts: Twin River (25); Silverbow; Clifford; Bellehelen; Revielle (100); Gold Center; Roses's Well; Leeland; Lodi; Jerrerson; Darrough Hot Springs; Quartz Mountain; Berlin; Arrowhead; Troy; Grant City; Ellsworth (76); Blue Eagle Springs; Morey; Moore's Station; Wahomie; Amargosa; Ray; Ione; Hot Creek (27); Spanish Spring; Monarch; Ophir Canyon; Millett; Park Canyon; Northumberland (50); Phonolite; Union; Grantsville; Stirling; Johnnie; Manse Ranch; Tybo (255); Fairbanks Ranch; Transvaal; Atwood; Pactolus; Cloverdale; Golden; Duckwater (50); Junction (14); Bonnie Claire; Gold Crater; Kawich; Barcelona; Smith's Station; Pine Creek; Baxter Spring; Central City; Jett; San Juan; Washington; Ellendale; Danville; Golden Arrow; Pioneer; Downeyville (25).

Ormsby (Carson City) County—Ghost towns and possible ghosts: Saint's Rest; Lakeview; Curry's Warm Springs; Clear Creek Station; Swift's Station; Empire City.

Pershing County—The old mining camp of Mill City, now merely a filling station on US 40-95, is 39 miles southwest of Winnemucca. Attendants at the Mill City filling station will give directions to the completely deserted mining camp of Star City.

After the discovery of its rich silver ore, Star City was the scene of one of the wildest booms in Nevada. In 1863, the town had 1,500 people, with two hotels, a Wells Fargo office, telegraph office and dozens of buildings. By 1868, the boom had collapsed, and the town was depopulated.

Pershing County—The almost deserted town of Oreana is on Interstate 80 about 37 miles north of Lovelock. Oreana was once a lively center for a lead mining district. Very little of it remains.

Pershing County—Inquiry should be made in Lovelock (Interstate 80) for directions to the place known as the Indian Hunting Grounds. Arrowheads, spearheads and other parts of Indian weapons have been found there in abundance.

Pershing County—The ghost town of Rochester is on an unnumbered road northeast of Lovelock where directions to its ruins can be obtained.

In the 1850's, silver was discovered at Rochester. When another strike was made in 1911, the camp grew rapidly to a population of 1,500. $10,-000,000 worth of silver was produced at Rochester. Only one building now stands amid the ruins of its foundations and cellar depressions.

Pershing County—Unionville is in the approximate center of the county on the east slope of the Humboldt Range. It is deep in Buena Vista Canyon and may be reached by an unnumbered road running west of State 50. Before Humboldt County was divided, Unionville was the county seat. Silver was discovered there in 1861. By the spring of 1863, the population of the community was growing by 20 a day. The town had 10 stores, 6 hotels, 9 saloons, 2 express offices, 2 drugstores, 4 livery stables, a watchmaker's shop, a brewery, mill, a school and a church. All these and many stone and adobe homes were scattered for a distance of two miles along Buena Vista Canyon.

Unionville's population reached about 3,000, but its decline began with the diminishing of its ore and the building of the railroad through to the west.

Today, the children of the neighboring ranchers attend school among the crumbling adobe walls of one of the oldest mining camps in Nevada.

Pershing County—In American Canyon about 12 miles south of Unionville, the last vestiges of a Chinese mining camp has disappeared, and even its name has been forgotten. Chinese were not welcome in most mining camps of the west, and they usually stayed to themselves in small colonies. Their mining activity in American Canyon began about the 1870's and lasted until 1900, though a few Chinese continued placering there until 1910. The last resident of the camp died in 1927. It is believed that the Chinese took $10,-000,000 worth of gold out of the canyon, but some estimates place the amount at twice that figure. The miners lived in dugouts or small rock cabins, and the community supported several stores.

Pershing County—Other ghosts and possible ghosts: Packard; Lima; Panama; Trinity; Vernon; Halfway House; Goldlands; Kennedy; Rabbithole; Rosebud; Rye Patch (65); Arabia; Poker Brown; Tarreytown; Aetna; Tunnel; Seven Troughs; Spring Valley; Humboldt House; Scossa; Humboldt City; Imlay; Farrell; Placeritas; Willard; Nightingale; Prince Royal; Lancaster; St. Mary's; Tungsten; Santa Clara.

Storey County—The ghost town of Gold Hill is very close to Virginia City, where inquiry concerning it can be made.

Gold Hill was born in 1859 when Old Virginia Fennimore and some of his friends discovered gold there. It was the first highly prosperous camp in the area. Loud, gaudy and facile in crafty dealing, it earned the nickname of Slippery Gulch. Two years after its founding, it was a booming city of stone and brick buildings, some of them three stories high. By 1862, the camp had a population of about 1,500. In addition to its mines and mills, it had stores, banks, saloons, hotels and theatres. With the discovery of the Comstock Lode its miners deserted to the new Golconda. Today, Gold Hill is a few tottering ruins, parts of brick or stone walls, and scattered piles of rubble.

Storey County—What remains of American City is one mile west of Gold Hill. From 1864 to 1866, this thriving town had two large hotels and other businesses. But the community never took root, and by late 1867 it had reverted to sagebrush. Remnants of its processing mill are all that is left of American City.

Storey County—The ghost town of Devil's Gate is about 3 miles south of Virginia City. Devil's Gate was never anything but a struggling village. It expired with the decline of the Comstock mines, and little remains of it today.

Storey County—The ghost of Six Mile Canyon lies two miles to the east of Virginia City. Built up largely by the excess of population from Virginia City, Six Mile Canyon prospered until the early 1900's when the closing of its last mill spelled its doom. Today, there is nothing to mark its site but stone ruins and mine dumps.

Storey County—Other ghosts and possible ghosts: Sutro (450); The Divide.

Washoe County—Directions to the Glendale Crossing of the Truckee River can be obtained in Sparks (Interstate 80). Sometimes called the Old Stone or Gates Crossing, Glendale Crossing was where much of the west-bound travel in pioneer days turned south through Truckee meadows. Many wagon trains camped on this meadow to decide whether to take the road to the north or the one to the south.

Washoe County—On US 395 four miles north of Reno there is a place called Black Springs. The original Black Springs was one mile south on the old Beckworth Road. It was a stagecoach station operated by John Black. Black and John Poe, cousin of Edgar Allen Poe, established a mining camp called Poeville in one of the rugged canyons running off the Peavine Summit just east of the California border. Now completely deserted and with few signs of its existence, Poeville is difficult to locate.

Washoe County—Massacre Lake is a large dry lake lying to the east of the small town of Yva (State 34-8A), where inquiry concerning it should be made.

In 1850, a large and well-equipped wagon train was attacked by Indians at Massacre Lake. The travelers rashly chose to leave their wagons and charge the savages. They drove off the redmen but lost 40 of their companions. Many relics have been found in this very remote section of Nevada.

Washoe County—Inquiry should be made in Gerlach (State 34) for directions to the ghost town of Leadville, 37 miles to the north. The town was founded with the discovery of lead-silver ore there in 1909. The peak years were reached in 1924 and 1925, and the decline began in 1940. Only the blacksmith shop and a few other wooden buildings still stand.

Washoe County—Forty-Nine Canyon lies at the eastern base of the Cascade Mountains near Yva (State 34-8A). The stone wall of the canyon is covered with names and dates chiseled by travelers as messages for those to follow that they had reached this point on the Applegate Cutoff. The camp there was a favorite one for west-bound wagon trains.

Washoe County—Franktown was on US 395 about 21 miles south of Reno. It was founded by Mormons in 1852. The community built up rapidly. But in 1857, in response to a call from Brigham Young, over 350 Mormon families sold their property and returned to Salt Lake City. Frankton, however, revived in 1860 when a 60-stamp mill was built to refine Comstock ores. The town began to decline after the mid-1860's with the diminishing of the milling and lumbering business. Only foundations and the Virginia & Truckee Railroad water tank mark the site.

Washoe County—Buffalow Meadows, near Gerlach, was settled in 1865.

The center of a stock-raising district, the town had a school and two hotels. It was all but dead when its post office closed in 1913.

Washoe County—The ghost town of Galena is now a skiing area. This Galena near Carson City should not be confused with another Galena in Lander County.

The ghost Galena was founded as a mining camp in 1860 and was so called because of the large amount of galena found in the region. The mining venture failed, and he camp was moved up the creek to become a short-lived lumber supply camp for the Comstock mines.

Washoe County—Near Galena above the Bowers Mansion, which is the chief landmark in the area, is the site of Ophir. A stamp mill crushed ore there from a Comstock claim also called Ophir. All signs of the mill have disappeared.

Washoe County—In the vicinity of Nixon (State 33-34) two small mining camps, each with two names, grew up around the district's most important mine. Pyramid City or Lower Pyramid was founded in 1876. Two miles above it was a smaller camp called Jonesville or Upper Pyramid. Both villages disappeared in the late 1880's. No ruins mark the site of Pyramid City, but at Jonesville several crumbling rock walls are accessible to those with high-axle cars. Directions to these walls can be obtained in Nixon.

Washoe County—The site of Jamison's Station is about three miles southeast of Sparks (Interstate 80). In 1852, a Mormon trader named Jamison established a station at that point as a rest camp for pioneers on their westward trek. Emigrant wagon trains stopped at Jamison's Station to relax for several days in preparation for the final struggle over the Sierras. Only rock foundations remain.

Washoe County—The ghost town of Crystal Peak is only a half-mile northwest of Verdi (Interstate 80).

Crystal Peak was founded about 1864. By 1868, it was a rowdy camp of about 1,500 people engaged in supplying the lumber required for building the Central Pacific Railroad across northwestern Nevada. When the railroad placed its depot facilities at Verdi, Crystal Peak rapidly declined. Today, only a few graves and disintegrating foundations mark the site.

Washoe County—The site of Junction House is indicated by a historical marker about three miles south of Reno (Interstate 80). Starting as a ranch, Junction House became a busy crossroads settlement when a number of toll roads converged there. The post office was known as Truckee Meadows, but when the railroad was built through the meadows, it took the name of Andersons.

TREASURE GUIDE

Washoe County—What remains of Washoe City is on US 395 about 18 miles south of Reno. As the seat of Washoe County from 1861 to 1871, Washoe City attained a peak population of about 6,000 and had an extensive business section. With the loss of the county seat to Reno, Washoe City declined to a population of 200 by 1880. Only one commercial building, a few dwellings and the old cemetery are extant.

Washoe County—The ghost town of Ophir is about 20 miles south of Reno. In 1861, a 75-stamp quartz mill and complex were built at Ophir, and the town grew to several hundred people. The decline of lumbering and mill activities in the mid-1860's, however, ruined the camp. In 1871, when the post office closed, the place had no more than 41 residents. Then the big mill was dismantled and Ophir died. Some of its walls stand now in a private field.

Washoe County—Other ghost towns and possible ghosts: Bristol (167); Jumbo; Auburn; Wedekind; Glendale; Sheepshead (40); Derby; Olinghouse; Brooklyn; Hunter's Station, later known as Mayberry's; Vista (26); Huffakers; Steamboat Springs; Magnolia House; Incline.

White Pine County—Inquiry should be made in Ely (US 50-93) for directions to the abandoned mining camp of Hamilton, originally called Cave City. At one time the seat of White Pine County, Hamilton had a population of 10,000 with another 15,000 in the mushrooming camps around it. The boom at Hamilton was one of the greatest the west had seen. It began with the discovery of silver on the slope of White Pine Mountain. A $55,000 courthouse was built, and the town boasted an opera house, a handsome church and an elaborate hotel. The decline that started in 1873 was far advanced in 1886 when a series of fires struck the town and wiped out most of its buildings. With the loss of the county seat to Ely, Hamilton was doomed. Only stone foundations, crumbling walls, ruins of mills, and depressions of cellars attest to its former opulence.

White Pine County—In January of 1868, the Hidden Treasure Mine was discovered in the White Pine Range of Nevada, precipitating one of the most fabulous mining stampedes in the west. Out of it developed a score of mining camps, including that of White Pine City, which was so close to Hamilton that it almost comprised a suburb.

In February of 1869, a reporter wrote: "Ten thousand men are here now, and 50,000 will be here by the first of July." White Pine City hardly attained that, but it did reach 25,000 before its decline began. The rich ores were on the surface, and when they were worked out, White Pine City was finished. Its people gradually drifted away to other camps.

White Pine County—The ghost town of Treasure City is three miles south of the ruins of Hamilton. Treasure City was a gold camp 9,000 feet high. Its population reached 6,000, and in 1869 there were 42 business establishments in the town. But the glowing promise of Treasure City was destroyed by fire. Though her mines continued to operate, the town was never rebuilt. By 1880, her population had dropped to less than 100.

White Pine County—Hamilton, White Pine City and Treasure City were only the richest of the mining camps that sprang up in the White Pine Range. Shermantown had a population of 7,000 that by 1880 had shrunk to a single family. The 6,500 people of Eberhart all drifted away. Swansea, Menken, Monte Cristo, California, Mammoth City, and Babylon disappeared with their riches, leaving hardly anything behind. Even the names and locations of numerous other silver camps have been forgotten.

White Pine County—Inquiry should be made in Ely for directions to the ghost town of Taylor in the Shell Creek Range. Taylor was born with the first discovery of silver in this region in 1872. Although the area was one of the richest silver producers in Nevada, Taylor's growth was slow. After 1883, however, the town began to develop rapidly, attaining a population of 1,500 with several stores, an opera house, seven saloons, three boarding houses and other business establishments. The demonetizing of silver spelled the doom of Taylor, and by 1890, it was reduced to a ghost town of but two families. Today it is deserted. As in other mining camps of the area, visitors have to be extremely careful of open mine shafts.

White Pine County—About 12 miles south of Taylor, also in the Shell Creek Range, is the ghost town of Ward, which was noted for its charcoal kilns rather than its mining. On the slope of the mountain stood rows of beehive kilns used to burn the wood to produce charcoal for the surrounding mining camps. The area is now a State Park.

White Pine County—Inquiry should be made in Ely for directions to the abandoned mining town of Osceola. Gold lodes were discovered there in 1872, and placer mines, in 1877. A small stamp mill was built in 1878, but the town died with the advent of hydraulic mining in 1880. So little is left of the camp that it is difficult to locate.

White Pine County—The near-ghost town of Cherry Creek is in the Egan Rance about 45 miles north of Ely. Between 1872 and 1883, this silver, copper, lead and gold mining camp had a population of almost 6,000. By 1893, the ores were depleted, and so was Cherry Creek.

White Pine County—An unimproved dirt road from Cherry Creek leads to the old mining camp of Egan Canyon, where silver ore was discovered by soldiers in 1863. When the ores gave out there, most of its buildings were moved to Cherry Creek. Near the abandoned mine are the ruins of the Egan Canyon Pony Express Station.

White Pine County—Near Egan Canyon is what remains of the town of Schellbourne, called Schell Creek when it was a relay station for the Pony Express. It was renamed Fort Schellbourne after troops camped there in the 1860's to protect the mails and travelers. The town became a mining camp for a short time after silver was found in the surrounding hills. When the ores showed poor results, Schellbourne's buildings were moved to the richer Cherry Creek district. The site is now part of a ranch.

White Pine County—The ruins of the Antelope Springs Stage Station lie to the northeast of Eureka on the old route between Elko and the ghost town of Hamilton.

White Pine County—Other ghost towns and possible ghosts: Cedar Creek (566); Reipetown; Kimberly; Veteran; Steptoe City; Blaine; Ruby Hill; Aurum; Siegel; Tungstonia; Cleveland; Cold Creek; Mineral City (150); Muncy; Seligman; Buck Station; Pogue's Station; Pinto Creek Station; Hunter; Piermont; Butte Station; Newark; Blackhorse; Minerva; Picotillo; Round Spring.